A STORY OF
GRACE

BEYOND THE IRON CURTAIN

PHIL METZGER
WITH TRUDY CHUN

GOLGOTA

©2014 by Phil Metzger
Published by Golgota, H-1073 Budapest, Erzsébet krt. 13., Hungary
email: budapest@golgota.hu

Printed in the United States of America.

ISBN 978-0-578-14306-4

For further information on Calvary Budapest, please visit:
www.golgotabudapest.hu

For further information on Calvary Chapel Bible College Europe,
please visit: www.ccbce.com

Cover and interior design: Timea Vass, Budapest, Hungary

Copyrighted pictures taken by:
p. 145, 153, 265 down: *Gábor Sebestyén*
p. 165, 177: *Tom Price, Calvary Chapel Magazine*
p. 189, 265 up: *Vivien Farkas*
p. 204: *Bertalan Fehér*
p. 245: *Megan Havelaar*
p. 264 up: *Nastya Alex Crook*
p. 264 down: *Blende Photostudio, Vác, Hungary*
Back cover: *Timea Vass*

*This book is dedicated to those
who are making disciples of all nations.*

*Thank you for allowing
God's story of grace to continue.*

CONTENTS

ACKNOWLEDGEMENTS

To my wife, Joy, whom I love with all my heart. Thank you for serving the Lord with me all these years and for putting up with so much. You are my hero. To Niki, Karina, Judah, and Hannah, thank you for letting your mom and me follow God's leading. You bring us so much joy.

To Trudy Chun, for all your hard work. This book has been in my heart for so long, and you helped me bring it to life. To Russ Chun, thank you for letting me steal so much of her time.

To Lisa Collins, who invested so much time and energy to editing. This could not have been done without you. To Árpád Horváth Kávai, John Blocher, Luann Doman, and all those who helped with editing and proofing this project, thank you. To Elisa Newberry for transcribing so many interviews, thank you for your diligence.

To all of you whom I interviewed for this book, thank you for letting your stories and perspective be shared with the world. Each one of you has had such an impact upon me over the years, and I am so thankful.

To the Hungarian people, thank you for letting us preach the gospel across this great nation. We pray for you and we love you.

To our God, who makes all things new.

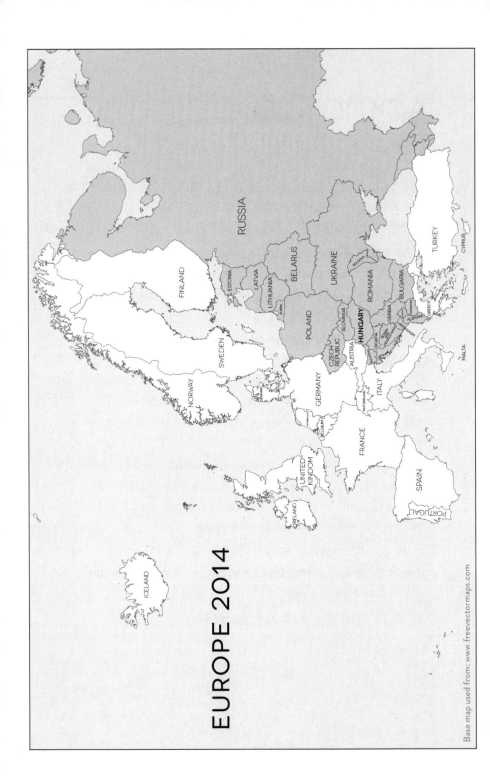

EUROPE 2014

ICELAND

FINLAND

NORWAY

SWEDEN

RUSSIA

ESTONIA

LATVIA

LITHUANIA

BELARUS

UKRAINE

POLAND

GERMANY

UNITED KINDOM

IRELAND

BELGIUM

FRANCE

SPAIN

PORTUGAL

CZECH REPUBLIC

SLOVAKIA

AUSTRIA

HUNGARY

CROATIA

SLOVENIA

ROMANIA

SERBIA

BULGARIA

ALBANIA

GREECE

ITALY

TURKEY

CYPRUS

MALTA

GOLGOTA (CALVARY) CHURCHES IN HUNGARY 2014

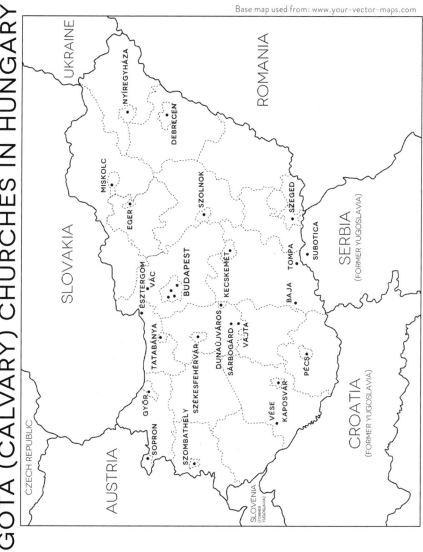

Base map used from: www.your-vector-maps.com

CZECH REPUBLIC

AUSTRIA

SLOVAKIA

UKRAINE

SLOVENIA
(FORMER YUGOSLAVIA)

CROATIA
(FORMER YUGOSLAVIA)

SERBIA
(FORMER YUGOSLAVIA)

ROMANIA

SOPRON

GYŐR

SZOMBATHELY

SZÉKESFEHÉRVÁR

TATABÁNYA

ESZTERGOM

VÁC

BUDAPEST

MISKOLC

EGER

SZOLNOK

NYÍREGYHÁZA

DEBRECEN

SZEGED

SUBOTICA

TOMPA

BAJA

KECSKEMÉT

DUNAÚJVÁROS

SÁRBOGÁRD

VAJTA

PÉCS

KAPOSVÁR

VÉSE

PREFACE

The story that I am about to tell is not new; it has always been God's heart. He has been working it out in the lives of His people for thousands of years. It is a true story that takes place in Eastern Europe at a time when the world was dramatically changing. Although I have lived and served in Hungary for the last twenty years, this is not my story. In fact, this is not the story of any one person. It is, however, a conglomeration of many stories which intertwine to tell one magnificent story of grace.

THE IRON CURTAIN

The stage had been set long ago when, in the wake of World War II, the Soviet Union raised an Iron Curtain that separated Europe into two distinct sectors: East and West. Hungary became an unwilling border country in this new political reality.

The Soviet machine worked hard to transform the landscape of Hungary, nationalizing businesses and restructuring society. By 1956, Hungarians had enough of Soviet tyranny. On October 23, they rose up against their Soviet oppressors. And even today, all across the land, buildings riddled with bullets testify of that remarkable day when a defiant people stood united in the face of oppression.

But the revolution was short lived. The Soviets lashed back with a crippling blow, killing more than 30,000 and driving hundreds of thousands to flee the nation. The millions who stayed faced the harsh repercussions of the communist regime. There was no such thing as grace in this world. The Soviets interrogated thousands and executed hundreds, leaving no one unscathed.

For forty hard years the communist experiment continued. Many believers lost their lives proclaiming the name of Jesus. Many church gatherings went "underground," and contraband Christian literature and teaching tapes became like gold to fledgling groups of believers.

In the public eye, religion was largely considered the domain of the elderly. Society taught the younger generations to believe the Church taught myths and fairy tales. It was a crutch for the weak. One Hungarian, Jani Németh, recalls having never in his life gone to church. In his Soviet-schooled mind, the very idea of God seemed ridiculous.

FREEDOM

Then in 1989, the Soviet empire fell apart, and Hungary soon emerged from its ashes as a democracy. Freedom was finally within its grasp. But true freedom will never be found in a political system or in economic reform. Neither will it be discovered in new religious ideas. True freedom is found only in Jesus.

The nation began to rebuild its identity, and from a political standpoint, this has been a success. Hungary has had peaceful elections since the fall of the Soviet Union. But political change does not magically dissolve darkness. Beneath the veneer of political transformation, the people still struggled with all the symptoms of the spiritually sick.

Many religious groups flooded into the land, promising solutions to these deeper problems. Every cult and false religion raced in with lightning speed. Soon Mormons, Hare Krishnas, Jehovah's Witnesses, and Scientologists preyed on a people desperately seeking some truth to hold onto in the wake of the failed experiment known as communism. But Christians also came, bearing a message of God's grace.

OUR STORY BEGINS

And that's where our part of the story begins. In the late 1980s and early 1990s, as the Iron Curtain fell, a California pastor sent a few people to go and see what the Lord would do in Eastern Europe. I was one of those people.

We went with our Bibles, guitars, and a desire to bring the truth of God's freedom to the nations. We talked to people on the streets and met in parks or small apartments. Through music, teaching English, or even riding skateboards, we used anything we could to show God's love and teach His Word. We were truly unlikely missionaries with unconventional methods. From the former drug-dealer to the California surfer, from the draft-dodger to the academic—we were all profoundly unqualified for the task at hand, and yet that is perhaps what made us the ideal people for the job. We would have to rely completely on God's grace to be able to share God's grace.

Somehow, the Lord managed to use us. People responded to God's love, discovering what relationship with Him is all about, and a church movement was born. It became known as Golgota (Golgotha).

As I write this book, I can count twenty-three Golgota churches across Hungary, eighteen in Ukraine and several across Serbia, Croatia, Romania, Slovenia, and Slovakia. No longer a "missionary endeavor," the movement is now mostly led by nationals across these Eastern European nations.

REDEEMING GRACE

Golgota was born not as the strategy of any one man. In many ways, it seemed to come about in spite of everyone involved. And it testifies that through adversity and despite sin, God is still redeeming people by His grace.

God's grace is what this book is all about. It's the story of a region that endured oppression and disillusionment and was hungry for grace—the kind of grace that has the power to awaken people out of an almost tangible darkness into a very tangible faith in Jesus.

Golgota is far from being the only church God is using in Hungary and in this part of the world. Many wonderful churches and Christians have served God mightily in this region long before we came, and they've done so under extremely difficult circumstances.

I hope that this book honors all those who came before us—those who understand firsthand what Christian persecution is all about. And I pray that it inspires those who will come after us to boldly preach the message of Jesus Christ and continue to carry the torch of God's great story of grace.

Grace is the thread of eternity
woven throughout human history.

Phil Metzger

1

THE IRON CURTAIN TEARS

The Spirit of the LORD God is upon Me, because the LORD has anointed Me to bring good news to the poor; He has sent Me to bind up the brokenhearted, to proclaim liberty to the captives, and the opening of the prison to those who are bound; to proclaim the year of the LORD's favor, and the day of vengeance of our God; to comfort all who mourn; to grant to those who mourn in Zion—to give them a beautiful headdress instead of ashes, the oil of gladness instead of mourning, the garment of praise instead of a faint spirit; that they may be called oaks of righteousness, the planting of the LORD, that He may be glorified.

ISAIAH 61:1–3

"Daddy, whatcha doing?" The little boy peered over his father's shoulder. The man, a pastor who had fled his homeland of Hungary some years before, sat hunched over his desk, painstakingly removing the fragile magnetic recording tape from the plastic cassette.

"I'm sending hope back to Hungary," he explained to his son. "You see, this is a recording I made of a Bible study in Hungarian for the people of my country." He thought often of old friends and family whose lives were being crushed in the spiritual barrenness of the Soviet Bloc.

"But why are you taking it out of the cassette?" the curious boy inquired.

The pastor sighed as his face grew sober. "People there aren't allowed to study God's Word like we are," he explained. "So I want to do whatever I can to help them." He gently pulled back the envelope lining and placed the celluloid-like tape between the layers. He worked with surgical precision. Then after replacing the lining, he inserted an innocuous letter in the envelope and sent it to his loved ones behind the Iron Curtain.

That letter would weave its way through the international postal system, through the hands of government censors, until it finally arrived at its humble Hungarian destination. There, in the secret silence of the late night hours, an unassuming Hungarian man would remove the contraband recording and thread it into an empty cassette. He would smile when the deed was done. It would be a smile of hope. For after he savored the sweet sounds of the teaching, he would covertly pass it on to others, who would in turn do the same. This was what the Christian life looked like in those dark years behind the Iron Curtain as communist laws sought to wipe faith from the very soul of Hungary.

Across the border in Yugoslavia, communism took on a different flavor. Not under Soviet tyranny, the society breathed a little more freely. But still, embracing faith or religion came with a cost.

"I want to take the children to be baptized," the concerned mother in Subotica, Yugoslavia told her husband in the late 1980s. She had foregone the infant baptism to avoid conflict years before. Now that the children were 5 and 10 years old, her own Catholic upbringing gnawed at her heart. She felt she would be failing them as a mother if she did not follow through on at least this one fundamental sacrament.

Her husband sighed deeply. This would be complicated. After all, he was a member of the Communist Party. He could not be a part of any such thing. It would be professional suicide. But there she stood before him with desperation in her eyes.

"Okay, okay," he finally gave in. "But do it when I am gone on business next week just in case anyone finds out." He looked at her with all earnestness. "I don't know anything about it."

In this world where faith and religion were so meticulously extracted from the public eye, something was beginning to stir. The faithful, both inside and out of these countries, never grew weary of praying for more of God's grace for this part of the world. For forty years, it kindled quietly, but in 1989, the spark began to ignite, and a light began to break through the tear in the Iron Curtain. Who would have thought that light would break into Hungary by way of its neighbor to the south, Yugoslavia?

THE WALL FALLS

But God chose what is foolish in the world to shame the wise; God chose what is weak in the world to shame the strong. (1 Corinthians 1:27)

The professor stood before the university class dumbfounded. "I don't know what to do or say," he mumbled. Last year, he had dazzled the class with his intellectual rhetoric regarding how Yugoslavia was neither a part of the Eastern nor Western Pact. He had ardently criticized capitalism while simultaneously shooting down the tyranny of Soviet-styled communism. But over the summer communism fell and with it the Iron Curtain.

For a professor of Political Ideology in Yugoslavia, the world must have felt like it was spinning out of control. He had written the textbook for the course. But now, in light of the summer's events, all he could do was stand before the class and say, "Nothing I wrote stands anymore."

There was a vacuum, a void, a huge chasm where communism once stood—and a haunting question of what could fill the emptiness. What could take its place? For adults it was a time of turmoil and confusion. But for the young it was a radical time of opportunity and options—to explore all that was once taboo. No longer blocked from investigating new ideas, the youth stood poised to bring their nations into this new world.

Young people were trying everything—both good and bad. Some, on whom God's Spirit was already beginning to move, began exploring faith. Szilárd Márkus, then a student at the technical university in Novi Sad, raced to any and all Christian services. He felt driven to go, simply because no one was there to forbid it. And he was not alone. Young people were searching for something more, something better.

It likely seemed chaotic as so many changes were happening so fast. But in the midst of that overwhelming sense of something failing, God was accomplishing His plan. Like a well-strategized chess match, God had already begun to set His pieces in place—even from halfway around the world. But sometimes the pieces were a little resistant.

TOO MUCH!

But He said to me, "My grace is sufficient for you, for My power is made perfect in weakness." Therefore I will boast all the more gladly of my weaknesses, so that the power of Christ may rest upon me. For the sake of Christ, then, I am content with weaknesses, insults, hardships, persecutions, and calamities. For when I am weak, then I am strong. (2 Corinthians 12:9–10)

"I can't do it! I just can't do it!" Brian Brodersen cried out to God. It was the spring of 1990, and he was scheduled to leave for Belgrade with an outreach team in a matter of hours, but he was falling apart. The pressures of pastoring his California church coupled with severe bouts of Chronic

Fatigue Syndrome left him crippled with exhaustion. He scarcely had the energy to get through the demands of daily life. How could he be expected to fly halfway around the world and minister to the people there?

What was worse was the fact that the whole trip was one haphazard disaster waiting to happen. They hadn't a clue where they would stay or exactly what they would be doing. People had told him he was crazy to go. He was beginning to think they might be right. It was like taking a shot in the dark and expecting to hit a target. And in his current condition, it was too much! "I can't do it!" he cried out again.

The tender words of his encouraging wife wafted in from the other room. "Shut up, you big baby! Just get dressed and go to the airport. You're going on this trip!"

Her words served as a wake-up call. For regardless of how miserable he felt, the fact was that God had arranged this trip. Brian sat back for a moment and remembered how he and his wife had met György and Melinda at the "Castle" in Austria about a year earlier. "You should come to speak in our village in Yugoslavia," György had said through a thick accent. "Maybe God will do something there."

The Castle was truly a special place. Purchased in 1989 by Calvary Chapel, the Schloss Heroldeck stood as a majestic structure built in 1912, overlooking the picturesque Lake Millstatt in Austria. During World War II, it caught the eye of Nazis occupying Austria, who seized it and turned it into a retreat center for the Third Reich. After the war, the Castle became a center for displaced and underprivileged children until 1988, when it was put up for sale. Calvary Chapel bought the property with a vision of using it to train future Christian leaders struggling to survive behind the Iron Curtain. Pastors and Christian leaders would come from the East to participate in Christian conferences and seminars. Western Christians would share, train, and learn from their Eastern counterparts.

The Castle in Austria

But when the church bought the property, no one suspected that within months, the Iron Curtain would tear apart, allowing the Castle to become more than a bridge. It became a free flowing conduit of ministry between East and West. Brian's connection with György and Melinda was just one of the many friendships forged at the Castle. Brian and György had exchanged contact information, but Brian thought that nothing would likely ever come of it.

It was the age before Internet and email, Facebook or iPhones. György and Melinda's village had one small phone booth, which served as the only phone for the whole community. All arrangements would have to be orchestrated through snail mail, and even that could be dicey. But somehow those critical handwritten letters made it through.

Countless times Brian had considered writing to the couple to cancel the event. But something inexplicable always diverted him from carrying out his intentions.

Despite his feebleness and fatigue, Brian knew his wife was right. He would have to rely on the grace of God moment by moment to have the energy to function, much less minister. He had to believe that God's grace would be sufficient to transform a sickly man into a tool for His own purpose. And so, he pulled himself together and headed for the airport where he met up with the rest of the team.

THE MIDDLE OF NOWHERE

Brian preaching (on right)

"Cock-a-doodle-doo!" The cry of the rooster cut the morning air in the small Yugoslavian village where Brian found himself. In the three days since he arrived with his team, the sound had become familiar. Pigs and other livestock wandered freely through the pothole-ridden roads. He felt like he was in the middle of nowhere.

The team had arrived at the village ready to share the gospel, ready to see God work His grace, only to discover that they really were not even wanted. György and Melinda had contacted all the local pastors, excited about the possibilities of awakening their sleepy village to what life can be in Christ. As the first rays of early morning sun slipped into the room where he slept, Brian reflected on their arrival.

After a heartfelt welcome, György had apologetically announced, "Well, that one pastor decided that he didn't want you to come," he stammered a little and then continued. "And the other church said that it probably won't work out."

The only church that would let them share was a Reformed church in a nearby village. There, with all the energy their jet-lagged bodies could muster, they had shared their style of praise and worship and talked about the grace of God through Jesus Christ. The crowd of fifteen elderly people sat as stone-cold statues. Not a smile or a grimace. No motion, no emotion. The team left the church feeling worse than when they had arrived. Had they really come all this way for nothing?

We've still got three weeks here, Brian sighed to himself. *We gotta do something else.*

SOMETHING ELSE

"Something else" came in the form of an excursion to two nearby cities: the border city of Subotica and across the border in the Hungarian town of Baja.

When the tall buildings of Subotica broke the horizon, the team brimmed with excitement. "Let's go here! Let's stop here! We want to go to that city!" After almost a week in the rural village, the Americans craved the possibilities a city could bring. "Yes! Yes! That's where we are taking you," György replied.

György had arranged for them to speak at a local Pentecostal church. After the service, someone had an idea.

"Let's go out on the streets and do some stuff," one of the Americans suggested.

"No, no. You can't do that here!" Tibor Varga, one of their hosts, exclaimed. The government's laws had left fear in his conscience.

"Sure we can," another team member added. "Let's do it!"

"Absolutely not!" Tibor insisted.

Then Taiwo, a member of the Pentecostal church, chimed in, "Yeah, we can do it. We can do it!"

And away they went. Using the church's instruments, the California crew set up on the streets and started jamming, creating such a spectacle that within minutes, more than fifty teens thronged around them. The kids all spoke English well, so nothing stood in the way of the gospel. That is, until the police arrived to break up the unauthorized gathering.

In the chaos that ensued, Brian grabbed one of the teens and said, "Meet us here tomorrow, and we can talk."

And so the Americans began to meet with the teens. The kids talked and asked questions and were fascinated by the concept of faith.

Music seemed to be key to reaching young people, so Brian and his team created a band and started playing the disco circuit around Subotica.

Fliers for this crazy American band flooded the streets. A California band in this part of the world drew young people like a magnet to metal. The concerts were punctuated by a gospel message and testimony of what life in Christ is all about. And countless young people who came to dance and party unexpectedly found a Savior.

BORDERLANDS

Eastern Europe is a big unknown to most in the West. Many Americans do not understand that the borders of these countries have moved many times over the last century and before. As a result, borders do not necessarily indicate ethnic and cultural divisions. The northern part of the former Yugoslavia (present day Serbia) is largely ethnically Hungarian, because these lands used to belong to Hungary.

Cities in this region often have two different names, one being Serbian and the other being Hungarian. The city that bears the Serbian name "Subotica" is called "Szabadka" in Hungarian, which means freedom.

A NEW ERA

Their days were filled with music, concerts, friendship, and fun. The California team became enraptured in what God was doing. But while they savored the experience, they never suspected they were actually pioneering a new phase of missions within the movement of Calvary Chapel. Up to this point, the hundreds of Calvary churches across the United States and overseas had developed their own missions programs or supported other missions agencies. The church partnered with wonderful groups like Campus Crusade, Youth With A Mission, Brother Andrew (who was smuggling Bibles), as well as a host of other organizations.

But now God had decided to start something new. And the focus was clear. While the ministries might include everything from youth outreach to orphanage work to prison ministry, Calvary Chapel was called to be first and foremost a church planting ministry—to bring people to Jesus and then to help them to grow in their newfound faith. That's not to discredit or dishonor the historic churches of any region. Each church has its place in God's plan. But not everyone fits into the traditional mold. And the Calvary style created a new option, a more casual packaging for the fundamental truths of Jesus.

SEEDS OF A NEW CHURCH?

For the rest of the month-long trip, the team spent time with these new believers hoping to help lay the foundation of faith in their lives. But a month does not last forever. Eventually the day came when they had to fly home.

Brian ached inside at the thought of leaving these teens. No church would accept them. No church would really meet them where they were.

You cannot abandon them! God pressed the sharp thought deep into Brian's soul. It was an uncomfortable reality. Brian took a deep breath and thought hard. *What could he do?*

Just before leaving, he called the young people, the new believers, together. He looked into their faces, so full of hope and excitement. He could not let this good thing die. "We have to go back to America," he said sadly. "But you guys keep coming here," he pointed to the place where the teens all hung out. "Bring your Bibles, pray with each other, and read the Scriptures together."

Perhaps at that moment Brian was not consciously thinking in terms of "church planting," but somehow instinctively he hearkened to the greatest church planting manual ever written. Acts 2:42 tells us: "And they devoted themselves to the apostles' teaching and the fellowship, to the breaking of bread and the prayers." He knew this had to happen if they were to spiritually survive.

Throughout the book of Acts we see the believers praying. They prayed for strength, for unity, for boldness, and for an outpouring of the Holy Spirit. They prayed alone and together, they prayed in prison and in home meetings. They prayed because they did not know what else to do. Prayer was not just some sort of religious requirement. It was their way of connecting with Jesus. He was the One saving and working. The new believers in Acts were as clueless as this bunch of teens in the city of Subotica, Yugoslavia. Just as those early Christians were rooted in Christ, so also this group of youth had to connect with the Lord in all things. It was not simply the act of prayer that made the church successful. Hearing from God, dying to self, and doing what Jesus told them was the key.

It was truly foundational advice, but would it be enough for these kids? They were like sheep without a shepherd. What would become of them? God gave Brian such a supernatural love for His church that he could not bear to turn away from these new believers in need of help. Brian knew that ultimately the development of their faith was a work of the Spirit of God, not his own handiwork. The Church, be it a large congregation or this small group of teens, belongs to Him. Still, God has commanded His people not to simply manufacture converts, but to make true disciples. And discipleship takes time.

In that moment, Brian made a commitment in his heart and a promise to a bunch of kids, "In one month, I'll send some people to come help you."

THE PROMISE

Four weeks earlier, Brian could scarcely drag himself on the airplane to come to this part of the world. He had felt no great longing for the souls of Eastern Europe. Now he could barely bring himself to get on a plane to fly home. The Spirit of God had clenched his heart for these kids and he would never again be the same.

As the plane lifted off from Belgrade, Brian gazed out the window at the clouds that speckled the distance, and he thought about his promise. Could a California pastor realistically find a group of Christians who were willing to drop everything to move to Eastern Europe? If so, would they be mature enough to disciple these young souls? And could all this happen in a single month's time?

Brian knew it was next to impossible. But he also knew a God who specialized in the impossible. He leaned back in his seat and prayed for those young people. For only by the grace of God would his promise ever be fulfilled.

2

WHO WILL GO?

I heard the voice of the Lord, saying: "Whom shall I send, and who will go for Us?" Then I said, "Here am I! Send me."

ISAIAH 6:8

"Hey guys, you want to go to Yugoslavia?" youth pastor, Richard Cimino, yelled to the young men hanging out at the high school offices of Calvary Chapel Costa Mesa. He leaned back in his chair, pointing at the phone, which still hung at his ear as he chuckled, "Brian wants to know if anyone is willing to go."

Mike Harris, the assistant youth pastor, smirked. "I don't even know what Yugoslavia is!" He pushed his long surfer locks out of his eyes as he looked around the room for a map. The truth was that he did not even know where to begin scanning the globe for this obscure, seemingly insignificant country. It was a good laugh for the small group of California youth ministers who knew more about "catching a wave" than communism in Eastern Europe.

But while the talk of Yugoslavia might have seemed like a joke to the rest of the office that day, the truth was that something was stirring in Mike's soul. Nobody knew that he sensed his time at Costa Mesa was coming to a close. No one suspected he planned to quit and had already lined up a lifeguarding job that was supposed to start in three weeks' time.

As his hand meandered over that map of Eastern Europe finally finding Yugoslavia, his mind and spirit began to wonder, *Could this be what God is calling me to?* An inexplicable ache welled up inside him. Was it possible to have such a longing for a land he had never known?

Mike called Brian the following day. "I'm ready to go to Yugoslavia," he said with eagerness in his voice, void of all doubt and hesitation. And by the end of the month, he was on a flight to Belgrade to stay for several weeks and see what God would do.

BERRIES AND CHICKEN GIZZARDS

Mike wandered through the Belgrade airport looking for someone, anyone who might have been sent to pick him up. The strange Cyrillic symbols on the signs seemed to press in on him, making him feel almost illiterate. Everything was so foreign.

"Hello, you are Mike, yes?" a voice with a heavy accent asked. "I am Romeo." Perhaps it was his white tennis shoes or the surfer t-shirt, but something made Mike easy to identify as an American. Romeo had been sent to meet him and bring him home to his village for the first two weeks. Romeo, along with Taiwo and Tibor, were the ones Pastor Brian had left in charge to minister to the new believers in Subotica until someone could get there to help out.

Rumbling down the Serbian back roads, Mike soon found himself settling in at Romeo's house in a quaint village about eight miles from the city of Subotica. He tucked his suitcase behind the dingy couch/bed in the corner of the stucco-covered, mudbrick house. This would be "home" for a while. He took a deep breath and sighed through his jet lag.

The clucks of a chicken would wake him in the morning amid the dogs' barking and the sounds of village life. For all he knew it was the same chicken whose gizzard he would be eating for dinner later that day. Life was simpler here and a little bit raw. Gizzards and berries comprised standard fare at Romeo's house. But for the $30 a month the host lived on, the giblets and fresh fruit amounted to a feast.

In-N-Out burgers and the beaches of Orange County were a world away and the California youth pastor was beginning to wonder what he had gotten himself into.

SUBOTICA: THE CITY OF FREEDOM

Three days after arriving, Romeo brought Mike into the city of Subotica. Mike felt a sense of relief to be back in urban civilization. The two men walked down the old streets of the scenic town. The buildings that rose up on both sides had witnessed both turmoil and prosperity in the past century: the rise of communism, the ascent of Tito, the artful evasion of Soviet dominance, and now a new era where no one knew what would unfold. Subtle rumblings of civil war, fear, and uncertainty hung in the attitudes and atmosphere all around.

Mike and Romeo emerged onto an area of parks, green with the scent of early summer. It was an area known to the city's youth as "Majmun plac," or the "Monkey Place." There teens gathered and gossiped, sitting along the narrow metal poles that made up the fences lining the parks. These grounds had served as a haven for youth for generations, since the days long ago when the cultured classes criticized the youth who hung like monkeys from the rails.

"Zdravo ste!" Romeo waved to a small group of three guys. "This is Mike from America."

"Can you translate for me?" Mike asked one of Romeo's friends. The young man agreed and so, Bible in hand, the young American began to preach the gospel to anyone who would listen. Soon a group of thirty youth had gathered, and the Spirit of God began to pour out His grace.

The following night, Mike preached again, and this time sixty people swarmed around him eager to hear his words of hope. The third night he returned, and this time eighty people thronged the Monkey Place. They were searching for something more than this life could offer; they were searching for a Savior.

God's Spirit moved with the speed of a tsunami and the former California surfer was riding its crest. It was as if the book of Acts was being lived out in the modern world. Mike knew he had to be in Subotica because it was there God saw fit to awaken the people to His grace. He spent Monday through Thursday of each week sleeping on a different person's couch. People were eager to host him, as they wanted to practice English and learn more about God.

The Monkey Place

MISSIONARY COMMITMENT

Not so long ago, becoming a missionary required a life-long commitment. Just the journey to reach a mission outpost took longer than a lot of modern missionary endeavors. Advances in transportation and technology have changed the face of missions, opening possibilities for short-term missions teams to contribute to the expansion of the kingdom of God. Short-term teams can bring a boost of energy to those committed for the long haul. Such trips also enable people to develop a heart for Christians who live a world away, expanding and intensifying prayer coverage in a region. However, short-term teams need to understand and honor the vision and advice of those who have years of experience under their belt, because the bottom line is that church planting in a foreign culture takes time, and therefore, the long-term commitment is key.

Pastors in America often say that the first five years of a church plant are more for the pastor than for the people. If that is true for churches at home, then in missions, even more years must be added. Language learning and cultural understanding do not happen overnight. It takes work and time. The people need to know the missionaries are committed and that they do not hold their native culture up as being superior. A critical part of being a missionary is simply being a humble learner open to discovering how another culture sees the world—without being a critic. It is only by learning how another culture perceives the world, God, and faith that missionaries can present the gospel in context. This is the way of love and grace.

TIME TO GO HOME?

Moreover, it is required of stewards that they be found trustworthy. (1 Corinthians 4:2)

God was pouring out His grace, as now oftentimes up to one hundred people would gather at the Monkey Place just to hear Mike teach about Jesus. The unassuming meetings had spiraled into nothing short of a "great awakening." But just as God began pouring out His Spirit, Mike's airplane ticket said it was time to fly home. He sighed sadly at the thought of leaving all of this at such a critical time.

He tried to think about home and all that he missed—California, fun in the sun, friends, and family. But it all paled in comparison to being a part of what God was doing in Subotica. He knew he could take no credit for it any more than a surfer can take credit for the perfect wave. He simply happened to be the one present and willing to be used by God. Mike understood that the privilege of being a part of all this came with a responsibility, a responsibility to be a faithful steward of what God had entrusted to him. In God's kingdom, nothing is more important than faithfulness. Talent, charisma, intelligence—they all mean nothing without it. Mike took his commitment seriously. He could not return to California and leave these young people without a shepherd.

I'm not going back, he determined. *I can't go back.*

TAKING THE TIME

Church planting takes time. How much? God does not create scientific formulas for such things. How much time depends on many factors because people groups are as diverse as the people themselves. Some missions agencies require a minimum five-year commitment due to the nature of the mission. For instance: Bible translation takes time and you cannot have people bouncing in and out after six months. Other missions agencies focus on supporting local pastors and use short-term teams to support ongoing native ministry.

As far as scholars can tell, the Apostle Paul was not in Thessaloniki for very long, and yet a church was established. Believers must remember that their hope is not in the commitment of a pastor but in the Holy Spirit. The church belongs to Jesus. He cares for people and He uses servants to faithfully express His love. Still, in modern society where everything is "instant" and "on demand," human nature tends to want to rush things. But God works according to His time frame, by His Holy Spirit. And He calls His followers to hear His voice and be faithful—no matter how much time it may take. Mike Harris and those who came after him understood this call to faithfulness.

BACK IN CALIFORNIA

Greg Opean paced around his office at Calvary Chapel Redlands. He had served as youth pastor in the church for the last two years and before that at Calvary Chapel

San Diego for three. It had been a good five years. But now, and for the last six months, his spirit had been unsettled. It was hard to explain. It was just a sense that he was in the wrong place and something had to change. He knew he had to resign.

Resign and do what? That was the pressing question for which he had no answers. He prayed again that prayer that had become like second nature. *God, where do You want me? What do You want me to do?* Greg sat down at his desk and began typing but was soon interrupted by his own thoughts. A surf company in San Diego offered him a job as a sales representative. *Well, that would be a change. But was it the right place?* The thoughts swirled around in his head as he finished typing up his letter of resignation.

Greg sighed deeply as he placed the letter on Pastor Don McClure's desk. His insides were spinning as his pastor picked up the paper and read.

A phone call interrupted the uncomfortable moment.

"Hey Greg, I know you are happy there in Redlands and I know this sounds crazy, but I had to call you." It was Brian Brodersen, and he was clearly enthusiastic about something. Greg listened to him with one ear while simultaneously watching his pastor and friend read his resignation.

"I just got back from Hungary a few weeks ago and your name has been on my heart," Brian continued. On the same trip where Brian discovered Subotica, he had also crossed the border and visited a Hungarian town called: Baja. There he had witnessed the same hunger for God's grace among the youth. "Greg, have you ever thought about being a missionary?"

The timing was uncanny. Greg stood slightly dumbfounded, but he did not want to rush in without the "okay" from above. "I'll pray about it," he responded.

He did pray about it, but in the meantime he got an offer to go and serve at a church in Oregon. It sounded like a dream come true, but as he tried to sleep that night the nagging in his heart left him tossing and turning. In those twilight hours, he knew God was saying no to Oregon.

As Oregon faded from possibility, Hungary burned stronger in his spirit.

JUST GO AND SEE

Jonathan said to the young man who carried his armor, "Come, let us go over to the garrison of these uncircumcised. It may be that the LORD will work for us, for nothing can hinder the LORD from saving by many or by few."
(1 Samuel 14:6)

Hungary? Could he really drop everything and just move to Hungary? That would be a big step, and Greg needed to know more before he could commit to anything. He went to meet with Brian.

"Okay, what's this thing about Hungary?" Greg asked after all the small talk. He expected Brian to have a clear plan all hammered out, but what he got was something quite different.

With a sparkle in his eye, Brian began to rhapsodize about how he had seen God's Spirit poured out during the outreaches in Hungary and Yugoslavia. "You know, the Lord is doing something," he said with a pastor's passion in his voice. "And I just feel like you're the guy to go—just to see what God will do."

That excitement was contagious.

Greg left the church building with a growing zeal in his heart for the obscure country on the other side of the globe. But what did this mean, "…just to see what God will do"? What did Brian really expect of him? It all sounded so inspiring, and Greg longed to be a part of a significant move of God, but he needed some hard facts.

He returned to Brian in search of those facts, needing to know the game plan. "Okay, you just said to go over and see what God does," Greg said pointedly. "What exactly is the job description?"

Again, Brian told stories of his experiences in that part of the world, how so many young people had come to Christ and needed to be discipled in grace.

"But if I go, what exactly do you expect me to do each day?" Greg pressed.

"You can lead worship, teach Bible studies, whatever!" Brian continued with the generalities. "Just go over there and see what God does."

Greg left Brian's office more interested in Hungary than ever, and at the same time more frustrated that there was no plan. He was not just some kid who could go across the ocean to "find himself." He was an adult, a college graduate with five years experience as a youth pastor under his belt. He had to know more before he could be expected to drop everything and move to Eastern Europe.

A third time Greg returned to Brian. When he walked in the door, the pastor just started laughing. "You are so called. Just go," he said as he put his arm on Greg's shoulder. "Dude, God is so doing this."

JUST GO

Greg woke up the following Monday morning still struggling with the whole proposition. And as the sun began to rise, his heart welled up inside him, and he cried out to God. *Oh Lord, I am so tired. I'm burned out after five years of youth ministry. I need some time to recover!*

God's voice spoke to him from the innermost parts of his soul: "Greg, I'm calling you to go."

Like puzzle pieces flying around that magically fall into place in an unexpected instant, it all made sense. God knew exactly how worn out Greg was in ministry. That is precisely why He was sending him to Hungary. Suddenly he would be in a world with no real expectations on him except to wait and "see what the Lord would do." He could truly rest in God's peace without the distractions of life that California held for him. God was not asking him to do something that would tear him down. This was a gift delicately designed to build him up. As Jesus said in Matthew 11:30, "My yoke is easy, and My burden is light."

As winter approached, Greg boarded an airplane for Munich. He was scheduled to spend a couple months at the Castle in Austria before setting out for Hungary.

STRANGE AND WONDERFUL

While Greg prepared to settle in Baja, Hungary, God was already working wonders forty-five miles southeast in

CONNECTED AND DISCONNECTED

One hundred years ago, when a letter was sent to a missionary, it would literally be months before they received it. Even twenty years ago in Russia, a missionary had to go to the post office to make an international call to the United States. Today a missionary can call, text, Facebook, tweet, or Skype home and get an instant response.

Things have changed, and for the most part it has been for the better. But for many missionaries this close digital proximity to home has prevented them from fully embracing that which God has called them to do. Here is where the danger lies.

Modern-day missionaries must untie the anchor to their own desires, opinions, and home. Not fully embracing the culture will leave their hearts torn between two worlds: the one growing ever better as the past becomes exaggerated in their imagination and the other growing ever worse by the realities of unfulfilled expectations.

Subotica, Yugoslavia. Mike poured his life into the youth who were seeking God. Everyday they would meet in the open-air park called the Monkey Place. School did not start until afternoon so they had Bible studies from ten in the morning until noon. Then they would meet again in the evening starting at eight. Mike spent as much time as he could on that square because for some strange reason, that is where God's Spirit was moving. The kids wanted to know more about Jesus, and nothing would stand in their way.

GUSTS OF GRACE

"Not by might, nor by power, but by My Spirit, says the LORD of hosts." (Zechariah 4:6b)

The wind whistled ferociously around the old wooden door of the tiny house where Mike now lived in Subotica. A local Baptist pastor had let him use his mother's place while she was away for the winter. And winter had come with a fury on this night. Mike stared out the window watching the snow and ice flying sideways in angry gusts.

"You ready to go?" asked Tibor Varga, who often translated for the unlikely evangelist. Evening visits to the Monkey Place every night had become a regular part of their schedule.

"Have you seen this weather?" Mike asked. "No one is going to be out there." In his mind, teaching outside in snowy squalls was inconceivable.

"I don't care," Tibor responded. "If one person comes then it's worth it."

Humbled by his friend's passion, Mike wrapped himself in a heavy coat and joined Tibor on this arctic expedition.

Blasts of frozen air cut into the men as they moved through town. The snow and ice pelted them all the way as they walked up the empty streets toward the Monkey Place. *There is no way anyone will be there,* Mike told himself as he shivered.

They arrived at the park and amid the snow and darkness stood about sixty kids huddled together, singing in the frigid night as they waited to hear more about Jesus.

The Californian stood shocked by the sight. If it had not been clear before, there was no longer any doubt. This was truly a move of God. It was not exported American Christianity with all its cultural trappings. Most Americans would never endure such conditions to hear a Bible study. This was God's hand moving in Yugoslavia. This was God pouring out His grace.

UNLIKELY MISSIONARIES

And the grace of our Lord overflowed for me with the faith and love that are in Christ Jesus.

1 TIMOTHY 1:14

"Bing! Bing!" The "fasten seat belt" sign flashed as the airplane shook due to unexpected turbulence. Greg Opean closed his copy of Charles Spurgeon's book *All of Grace* that he had been perusing on the flight. He peered out the window and between the clouds caught his first glimpse of the European continent. He leaned his head back on the headrest and let out a long breath. *We've come a long way together in a short time, Lord,* he prayed.

While this was true geographically, that's not what he meant. Greg's mind wandered back to his memories of years past. He remembered the first time he ever thought about faith.

"Hey Greg! What religion are you?" a friend had asked him when he was a sophomore in high school. He had no idea how to answer. He went home and asked his parents. That's when he discovered his mother was Catholic and his father was Jewish. It was the first time the issue had ever come up in his household.

Greg shook his head, slightly embarrassed, as he recalled the first time he ever set foot in any kind of church, a Catholic mass with a high school buddy. Clueless to religious culture and etiquette, he inadvertently committed Catholic sacrilege when he spit out the distasteful communion wafer and wiped it on the pew in front of him. He was promptly asked to leave.

Later in high school, he had attended a Young Life camp where he started actually listening to the "God speeches." Of course, the camp captured his attention with a lot of other attractions too, including the cool music, minibikes, and horseback riding, not to mention the really pretty girls.

He thought of the first time he saw Pastor Chuck Smith, founder of the Calvary Chapel movement, preaching verse-by-verse with a genuineness that gripped his very soul. "I want what that guy has!" he had said to himself, leading him to explore more of Christianity. As a result he had started attending a Bible study.

Poised to begin university, he hesitated to make any sort of commitment to Christ. He needed to see what was out there first. At the University of San Diego, Greg began to notice that virtually all his professors talked about God. Many were grappling with Him, and some were simply taking potshots at Him. But one way or another, it seemed that everyone Greg knew was either worshiping or wrestling with God on some level. God seemed to be everywhere, pushing Greg to choose which side he would be on. Finally, one day he made that choice.

"I want to worship You, Lord, with my life, not wrestle and fight against You any longer," Greg had prayed.

God lost no time in training Greg. First through Campus Crusade ministries and later by living with five guys in a ministry house on the beach, Greg learned first-hand what ministry was all about. At the ministry house, the young college student had learned how to come along-side homeless men and help them get back on the right track with God and society.

Greg's thoughts were soon interrupted by the pilot's voice on the intercom announcing the upcoming landing. As he felt the nose of the plane dip, he took a deep breath. His adventure would soon begin. He really had no idea what to expect. He was a youth pastor, not a missionary. Was he really prepared for what lay ahead?

After claiming his baggage and walking through customs, a shaggy-haired, blonde man approached him.

"Greg?" he said with uncertainty. "Are you Greg Opean?"

Greg nodded.

"The Castle sent me to pick you up." The young man smiled a welcoming grin. "I'm Rod Thompson."

Rod helped Greg load his bags into the vehicle, and soon they were racing down the highway. Since Greg's accommodations in Hungary would not be ready until February, he had been sent to the Castle for a couple months.

FAMILIAR FACE

"What is a friend? A single soul dwelling in two bodies." (*Augustine of Hippo*)

Rod and Greg

"Dude, don't I know you from somewhere?" Greg asked Rod as they sped down the highway.

"Yeah, you look really familiar to me too," Rod answered. He took a moment to study Greg's face, and then quickly turned his eyes back to the road. "Where'd you grow up?"

The two young men traced their upbringing as they traversed the German and Austrian countryside. Soon they discovered that they had actually attended the same junior high and high school together.

"Yeah, yeah, I do remember you now," Rod said. "You used to hang out with that guy, Jeff Crowson."

"He was my best friend in high school!" Greg laughed, remembering the good ol' days as the snowcapped mountains in the distance reminded him of just how far he was from the California beaches of home.

"He was my best friend in junior high!" Rod responded and then grew slightly sober. "He kinda ditched me for a cleaner crowd when I got into drugs."

"Well, neither of us knew the Lord back then," Greg commented, "I guess He's brought us both a long way." He smiled as he gazed out the window.

You have no idea just how far, Rod thought as his mind drifted back to those dark days years before.

A TEAM FOR HUNGARY

A plumber by trade, Rod had come to help with renovations at the Castle. The 1912 structure was indeed in need of a plumbing overhaul. Rod had been working there for some time, but meeting up with Greg stirred in his heart a latent desire to go into the former Eastern Bloc with the gospel. During Greg's stay, the two men began to pray together specifically for a move of God's Spirit in Hungary.

Greg noticed the plumber's passion for Hungary growing as they prayed. He could not help but think, *This guy should be serving on the mission field in Eastern Europe, not piecing together pipes in an old castle.*

"Hey Rod," Greg stopped him as they passed in a corridor one day. "Why don't you come with me to Hungary?"

Rod's heart welled up inside him at the possibility. Having served at the Castle for six months (since the summer of 1990), he found himself uniquely positioned to witness the dismantling of the communist system. It was the end of an era of oppression and had the potential to be the beginning of an era of hope. Hope and grace. These concepts became tangible in the stories coming out of Yugoslavia where God was using Mike Harris as His tool to reach a people who so desperately longed for a Savior.

It was all so incomprehensible for Rod. A child of the Cold-War era, his only glimpse into this strange and mysterious part of the world came through the 1984 Olympic games in Sarajevo, Yugoslavia. Could he really be among the first crossing the borders that once made up the Iron Curtain in order to share the gospel? Was a common plumber even qualified for such a mission?

Though his doubts may have loomed, his heart burned with a passion that could not be denied. Finally, he sat down to have a talk with the Castle director, Fred Boshaw. Fred assured him that as long as he finished his current plumbing projects, the Castle would wholeheartedly support his desire to join Greg.

SCHOOL OF HARD KNOCKS

For at one time you were darkness, but now you are light in the Lord. Walk as children of light. (Ephesians 5:8)

"The Spirit of the Lord is upon me, because He has anointed me to proclaim good news to the poor. He has sent me to proclaim liberty to the captives and recovering of sight to the blind, to set at liberty those who are oppressed."
(Luke 4:18)

Rod had been through so much in his life already. Smoking pot with his mom and doing cocaine with his dad since he was 16 years old, Rod had all the makings of a first-class felon. Although a plumber by occupation, which earned him $900 a week, he kept a sideline business dealing drugs to support his cocaine addiction.

One morning in 1983, after forty-eight hours of no sleep, the strung-out plumber headed to work from the place he had partied the night before. Realizing he had a little cocaine left over from his last trip, he struggled to smoke it in his freebase pipe. But his hands would not cooperate. They trembled uncontrollably.

He pulled over to the side of the road, determined to make it work. His breathing became labored like he was running a marathon as he tried to force his shaky hands to chop up the drug so he could just snort it instead. But he could not even coordinate his hands well enough to crush the coke. The chunks were too big. It would be like inhaling rocks. His eyes began to tear in frustration. He had to have it. He had to have it!

And then as Rod sat in his truck—red-eyed, sweaty and trembling—something happened. It was like a mirror came down from heaven, and he could see himself for the pathetic, desperate creature he had become. He knew he was killing himself and he did not want to die. Tears poured from his eyes as he cried out in something like a prayer, even though he had always said he was an atheist. He knew he needed help, supernatural salvation, and deliverance. He craved grace of the deepest kind.

Through a twelve-step rehab program, he managed to conquer his drug addiction. About a year and a half later, Christians began to witness to him, and he decided to check out a church, South Coast Community Church in Southern California. Then one of his friends invited him to attend a service at Calvary Chapel Costa Mesa, and that was where he met his Savior, Jesus. Indeed, in this school of the hardest knocks, God had shined His gospel of grace.

VELVETEEN RABBIT

When Greg looked at Rod, he was reminded of the children's story, *The Velveteen Rabbit*. Like the stuffed animal in the timeless tale, Rod was a bit rough around the edges. He was well worn; any measure of previous refinement and polish had long since disappeared. But just as the little girl in the story loved her rabbit so much that it became real to her, God had shown a supernatural love to Rod that made him completely genuine. He was the "realest" person Greg had ever known. And Greg felt honored to call him "friend."

Rod had never attended seminary or even Bible college. He had no degree or even significant ministry experience. He was just a previously drug-addicted plumber who had been transformed by God's grace. And perhaps that is exactly what made him profoundly qualified for this job. He knew all too well the bitter taste of hopelessness; he knew what it was like to be at the end of one's rope. And he also understood that those who have reached true brokenness are somehow uniquely equipped to embrace a deeper grace.

REMEMBERING THE PROPHECY

Rod stared out the window of the Castle as his mind wandered back to California. He remembered when his Swedish friends had talked about some Swedish prophet coming to town. A bunch of them from the home group decided to go check the guy out.

It had been a particularly low time in Rod's life, full of doubt and confusion. He had just returned to California after spending two weeks at the Castle in Austria, and during that time he felt that God was calling him to missions. But since returning to California, he had begun to wonder if it was all just some sort of pipe dream. He had applied to return to the Castle to serve but had not yet received a response.

The Swedish prophet spoke on going into your closet to pray. He explained how God knows each person's deepest desires, and that message pierced Rod's soul. It was as if he was the only one in the room, and the prophet spoke directly to him.

Rod had prayed, "God, please give this man a word of prophecy for me because I need to hear from You." And almost immediately, the man put a chair in the front of the room and asked if anyone needed prayer. Rod jumped into the seat without hesitation, and the Swedish prophet began to pray and prophesy over him.

"You will preach to the nations," he said. "You are God's ambassador to the world."

Others from their group also received prophecies regarding details of their lives that this guy could not possibly have known anything about. It all seemed to confirm God's call on Rod's life.

Encouraged by the prophet's words, Rod moved to Europe six months after this event. The Lord seemed to be bringing that prophecy into reality. He was going to be a missionary in the former Eastern Bloc.

ENTERING THE EAST

"The people who walked in darkness have seen a great light; those who dwelt in a land of deep darkness, on them has light shone." (Isaiah 9:2)

As the novice missionaries and their driver crossed over the border from Austria into Hungary, they felt as if they had stepped back in time. It was a world where villages still featured horses and wagons as a primary form of transportation and cars were tiny metal matchboxes lumbering down the bumpy roads.

Eight hours into the trip, their van finally passed the road sign for Baja and they found themselves pulling into a dreary, gray town. A series of colorless, time-worn communist block apartment buildings rose up on the right. As the van drew nearer, they could make out the graffiti marring the side of an already ugly building. The word "slums" rang through their minds, although no one said it aloud. But the building looked like the kind of ghetto you would find on the South Side of Chicago.

"Hey, Greg! That's where we're going to live!" Rod joked. And Greg laughed, making some comment about livin' in the hood.

It was all very funny until they met their contact in Baja and she brought them to their apartment, right back in the center of what they had thought was the ghetto.

The two young men realized that American-inspired expectations would have to take a backseat to the reality of life in the East, as they unloaded their van and dragged their stuff up the creaky, metal stairwell and into their tiny apartment.

DAYS OF REST AND READING

The first days passed slowly. The long nights of winter and endless gray days proved conducive to lots of sleeping, reading, studying, and prayer—the pillars of their first weeks in Baja.

"You ever feel like we dropped off the face of the earth?" Greg asked Rod one day. The missionaries laughed together. The bleak surroundings could not dampen spirits so bathed in the Word. Daily life became their own mini-seminary as they poured themselves into the Word. They would roll out of bed in the morning and start praying together and without even realizing it, they would spend countless hours before the throne of God.

As they studied the Bible both together and alone, a single theme kept emerging. There seemed to be no way to avoid it. It was as if the pages of Scripture silently screamed with such clarity that it could not be avoided or overlooked. It was the theme of grace.

BAPTIST BROTHERS

"The nation lives through its language."
(Count István Széchenyi)

"Sziasztok!" Rod and Greg showed off their Hungarian as they entered the home of the Hetényi family, removing their shoes at the door. The visits with the Hungarian Baptist pastor and his family had become a regular part of their day. It was a home away from home, bursting with warmth and good cooking. But this home was not simply a source of fellowship and sustenance, it also served as an informal school of culture and language.

Teaching them the basics of the Hungarian language, the family's children had become their first language teachers. And over the course of the afternoon, Greg would pull out his guitar, filling the small apartment with sounds of praise. Soon the children asked to learn how to play the instrument and in this process of teaching and learning in an atmosphere of love, eternal friendships blossomed.

One night as they made their way home from visiting the Hetényi family, some teens on the street caught a glimpse of Greg's guitar. They started talking to him and pointing at it.

"I don't understand what you're saying!" Greg responded. "I am American. Amerikai vagyok." He stumbled through some Hungarian that the Hetényi kids had taught him.

"You speak English?" one of the kids asked. "You have a guitar. What songs do you know?"

Greg smiled widely and looked at Rod. He pulled the guitar out of its case and started strumming. They sang together and within minutes about fifty young people had gathered around them. The two novice missionaries just started laughing. In the midst of this crowd, they felt like rock stars.

It had been only one month since the last Russian troops pulled out of Baja. Americans were as rare in this part of the world as palm trees in the Arctic. A fascinating novelty, the Californians found themselves uniquely positioned to be a voice that people would listen to in their search for something meaningful.

Between songs, the youth would ask questions through the one kid who spoke English. Finally, someone asked the question they had been waiting for.

"Why are you guys here?" the boy asked curiously.

Hearkening back to Brian Brodersen's words, they answered, "We're just here to see what God wants to do."

Eyebrows furrowed at the strange and unexpected answer. "So what are you? Priests or something?" shot back the next logical question.

Rod and Greg burst out in laughter. The very thought of the other donning a black robe and a white collar bordered on ridiculous.

"No, no we are definitely not priests," Rod clarified. "But we do want to help people know Jesus."

"Hey, if we started a Bible study would any of you want to come?" Greg interjected.

The young men looked out over the crowd after the question had been translated and their mouths fell open in disbelief. Fully fifty hands raised in the dark night air. Every person there wanted to know more about a God who would bring a couple of Californians to Baja, Hungary. Everyone wanted to learn more about Jesus.

GOLGOTA

And He went out, bearing His own cross, to the place called The Place of a Skull, which in Aramaic is called Golgotha. (John 19:17)

From punk rockers with crazy hair to the unwanted children of the streets, the youth just kept coming, longing to hear more about a God who would pour out His grace on even them. They ached to know more. Soon one Bible study was not enough, so they did two.

Pastor Hetényi smiled as he watched God move. He understood that this was bigger than any one denomination.

"Greg," he called the young missionary aside one day. "I know you came here to work with me and the Baptists." He motioned for Greg to take a seat. "But the truth is that some of these kids will never be comfortable in a traditional Baptist church. God is doing something new here."

Greg wondered where this conversation was leading. "So what do you think we should do?"

"You need to start something totally new, with a new name, and a new identity."

The wheels in Greg's visionary mind began to spin. "So you mean like a Calvary Chapel Baja?"

The pastor nodded.

"I guess we could call it *Kálvária Kápolna*," Greg thought aloud. That was the direct translation of the name. Greg had become increasingly skillful with the Hungarian language during his months in Baja.

"No, no, no! You can't call it that!" The pastor was emphatic, almost horrified.

"Why not?" Greg responded. "Isn't that the translation of 'Calvary Chapel'?"

"Well, perhaps literally," explained the Hungarian pastor. "But to the Hungarian mind, a *kápolna* is one of those church buildings you find in the middle of the cemetery."

"You mean like a funeral home?" Now Greg, too, felt a little horrified.

"And *Kálvária* is a morbid word that speaks about a life filled with suffering," the pastor continued.

"Definitely not a good church name," Greg reflected.

"I think you should call it *Golgota*." The pastor sat back in his chair enjoying the sound of the name.

"*Golgota?* As in Golgotha, the Place of the Skull?" Greg asked doubtfully. "Isn't that almost as morbid as 'funeral home'?"

"No, no, in Hungarian *Golgota* is really quite poetic," Pastor Hetényi explained. "Trust me, *Golgota* is perfect!"

4

CREATIVE
METHODS

And when Jesus heard it, He said to them, "Those who are well have no need of a physician, but those who are sick. I came not to call the righteous, but sinners."
MARK 2:17

"Hey, let's go out to some bars tonight!" Mike laid back on the red carpet in Greg and Rod's Baja apartment. Mike often came up from Subotica for fellowship and prayer. The men had just prayed and worshiped God for over an hour, and this was the last thing the other two expected to come out of Mike's mouth.

"Bars?" Greg asked.

"Dude! Can you think of a better place to tell people about Jesus?" Mike asked casually. A passion to evangelize consumed the California surfer-turned-missionary. Drunks and the dregs of society attracted him, not like bees to honey, but more like a physician to the sick. Bars and clubs sucked in the desperate and pacified them with mind-numbing booze. What better place to preach the gospel, to be God's tool to fill these empty lives with the all-consuming grace of the Holy Spirit.

BAR HOPPING

Empowered by God, Mike evangelized with a boldness that took Greg and Rod into places they had never thought to go. The surfer's broad shoulders and long hair commanded attention from the moment he walked into these seedy places. With boldness, he would stand surrounded by the stench of smoke and alcohol. Going eye-to-eye with evil, Mike would speak God's Word with power, and it resonated with a relevance that struck at a broken man's very soul.

Greg and Rod would stand back and watch God work. The young evangelist's passion and his boldness to storm the strongholds of Satan without hesitation challenged them to likewise reach out in faith. A critical catalyst at a significant time in human history, Mike inadvertently schooled his friends in this unconventional academy of evangelism where clubs made up the classrooms and lessons came on the far side of a lager.

FEAR AND FAITH

Whether we like it or not, fear is a factor in all our lives. And that's not always a bad thing. Fear of punishment often keeps a child from making wrong choices. Fear of going to prison may keep adults from committing crimes. But fear can also keep people from realizing the potential God has placed within them.

Fear can also paralyze. It can freeze people in their tracks like a deer in the headlights. Many Christians are terrified to share their faith for fear of rejection. Others are afraid of giving God control of their lives because of what He might do with them once they surrender. This fear of surrender to God keeps Christians from enjoying the blessings of obedience and submission.

Sadly, this fear factor has corrupted our perspective as we have come to believe the Christian life is all about "us versus them," a battle between the sinners and the saved. But when it comes to the human race, there are no good guys and bad guys, only sinners in need of a Savior. The Bible says, "For all have sinned and fall short of the glory of God" (Romans 3:23). But that is not the end of the story. God, who is rich in mercy, has made restoration possible through His sacrifice on the cross. We can be restored to God through Jesus our Savior.

God has assured us that we are "more than conquerors" and has promised us that nothing "will be able to separate us from the love of God in Christ Jesus our Lord" (Romans 8:37–39). Christ defeated the devil, death, and hell at the cross. If we are in Christ, our past is forgiven and our future is secure. If we believe this, then why do we live in fear of men? Why do we shudder at the thought of sharing our faith because of what someone else may think of us?

Maybe we've got it all backwards. Perhaps, the world and all the evil and darkness in it should fear us. Jesus told us that we are salt and light. We have received the gospel of grace. The gospel is God's power unto salvation. Jesus has already overcome the world, and we belong to Him.

Fear does not have to dominate our spiritual life. The Bible tells us that "perfect love casts out fear" (1 John 4:18). We must allow God's love to flow through us so that fear is no longer a factor, paralyzing us into inactivity for Him. When His love becomes the dominant factor, we can clearly see that there should be no "us" and "them"—only a world of people in need of a Savior.

RAGTAG CREW

For consider your calling, brothers: not many of you were wise according to worldly standards, not many were powerful, not many were of noble birth. But God chose what is foolish in the world to shame the wise; God chose what is weak in the world to shame the strong; God chose what is low and despised in the world, even things that are not, to bring to nothing things that are, so that no human being might boast in the presence of God. (1 Corinthians 1:26–29)

The Baja apartment became an unlikely oasis of friendship, fellowship, and fun as Mike made his visits on weekends, and other Americans hoping to minister, either long-term or short, sacked out on the floor of the tiny abode.

Sometimes up to six guys filled the floor, sleeping on makeshift pallets. With no room to even walk around, the guys laughed and prayed together as they watched and waited for God to work. Unlikely as it seemed, God had dropped this motley crew into something that felt like the book of Acts—where it seemed nobody ever knew what would happen next.

‘A CRY FOR HELP

And a vision appeared to Paul in the night: a man of Macedonia was standing there, urging him and saying, "Come over to Macedonia and help us." (Acts 16:9)

"Tap! Tap! Tap!" It was late in the morning when the knock came at the apartment door. Greg stumbled over the men sleeping on the floor. Hair all askew, Greg pulled open the door, not even taking time to dress.

"Are you the missionaries from Calvary Chapel?" the slender man asked in a distinct British accent. By this time the other guys had gathered around Greg in an array of bed head and boxers, wondering what was up with this British guy.

But the guy was not British at all. A Hungarian with a talent for language, the man reiterated his question, "Are you with Calvary Chapel?"

"Yeah, we're the missionaries," Greg said, perhaps realizing how unmissionary-like they must have looked at that moment.

The man began to weep uncontrollably right there in the doorway. As the tears poured from his eyes, Greg stepped back, a little shaken by the drama. *Oh no, this is someone with psychological problems,* he thought to himself.

Finally, the stranger managed to choke out some words between his sobs. "My name is Karl Elekes, and I am from Szeged," he said. "I have been listening to Calvary Chapel's shortwave broadcast out of England for almost a decade and praying—praying that you would come here and teach the Bible the way you do, verse-by-verse."

Greg invited the man into the already overpopulated apartment and had him sit down. He got him a glass of water while the man struggled to compose himself. "I have a small group of six people who come to study the Bible," the man explained. "Please come and help me disciple these kids." The stranger's eyes grew large as he pleaded, still swimming in his tears.

Rod, along with newcomer Paul Lange, would answer this desperate cry and within months a small church was born in the border city of Szeged, Hungary.

SPIRITUAL BATTLES

Be sober-minded; be watchful. Your adversary the devil prowls around like a roaring lion, seeking someone to devour. (1 Peter 5:8)

Finally, be strong in the Lord and in the strength of His might. Put on the whole armor of God, that you may be able to stand against the schemes of the devil.
(Ephesians 6:10–11)

STARTING FROM SCRATCH

In Golgota, church planting has often looked like this—someone has contacted the church because they are interested in having a Bible study in their city. God raises up a person, or preferably a team, to go to that city with the intentions of planting a church. It does not always happen this way. It is neither a formula nor our "strategy." That is just typically how it has happened.

That group then begins to share the gospel as often as they can. They start building relationships in the community. They work to strengthen those believers who are already interested in the Lord. And they strive to see those believers get a heart for their community. In those early days, months, and years, "church" is not about hiding away in a small rented room once or twice a week. Church is about hitting the streets with evangelism and building relationships.

As God saves people the fellowship grows. Golgota believes that the purpose of every church is to be a light to the community; not a stalwart of the faith hidden behind four walls. Being where the people are is critical because it is in the outdoor markets, the bus stops, the bars, and schools where you really begin to learn the heartbeat of a community. Church is not about getting people to come to your event on Sunday morning. It is about sharing the life of Christ with whomever God brings across your path.

Subotica, Baja, and then Szeged. God was pouring out His Spirit. But while these days were chock-full of God's power, the Enemy would not give up without a fight. After months of living together, Greg and Rod sensed the heaviness of the spiritual battle in their relationship with one another. They were easily irritated, they misconstrued comments, and at times just did not get along with each other. The spiritual blitzkrieg became so predictable that in time, they simply started expecting it.

"So who's the demon on today?" they would ask each other in the morning. They knew all too well that one or the other would be the center of Satan's attacks, and they had to fight the evil with patience and prayer. Occasionally they would hit a day when both suffered as targets of Satan's fiery darts—truly brutal days when all seeming success appeared to crumble around them. Still, God's light would eventually break through the darkness as the men cried out to Him.

SERVICE AND SALVATION

"Behold, I am doing a new thing: now it springs forth, do you not perceive it? I will make a way in the wilderness and rivers in the desert." (Isaiah 43:19)

Just as in the days of the early church, Christian service was not reserved for those with seminary degrees and academic accolades. Some even started serving before they came to know Christ.

"Hey Árpi, this team from Albuquerque is coming. Why don't you come help out?" Árpi Horváth Kávai was a 19-year-old in Subotica who had been coming to the church for only a few weeks. He had just begun to explore these concepts of God and grace. But Árpi had a sharp mind and a natural talent for language. When Mike Montgomery arrived with a team from Calvary Chapel Albuquerque, New Mexico, Árpi seemed the logical choice to serve as their translator. He started translating for them on the streets and as these ideas of salvation and sacrifice reworked themselves in his mind from one language to another, the Spirit of God began to pierce his soul. When he stood on stage translating someone's testimony after a musical performance, his heart reeled within him.

I don't even know the lingo, I don't understand the expressions they use, he struggled within himself. *All I know is that I have to make a decision here.* And Árpi made that decision by the end of the outreach.

It was certainly not evangelism by the book, but however unconventional, God chose to use even the unsaved to bring salvation to the lost in Eastern Europe.

CRITICISM AND CREDIBILITY

To the Jews I became as a Jew, in order to win Jews. To those under the law I became as one under the law (though not being myself under the law) that I might win those under the law. To those outside the law I became as one outside the law (not being outside the law of God but under the law of Christ) that I might win those outside the law. To the weak I became weak, that I might win the weak. I have become all things to all people, that by all means I might save some. I do it all for the sake of the gospel, that I may share with them in its blessings.

1 CORINTHIANS 9:20-23

"You don't know us; you're just some rich American! You're going to get back on a plane and go back to your rich lifestyle," a man barked at Mike Harris as he tried to tell him about his need for a Savior. "You don't know us. You know nothing about us. Why should I listen to you?" The man threw up his hands and walked away.

An ache clenched Mike deep in his spirit as he silently prayed for the man. So many had welcomed Christ eagerly in Subotica. But not everyone had a heart ready to receive the precious gift of grace. The residue of communism still stained society's soul with a fear of faith.

Still Mike, along with his main translator, Tibor, and others committed to sharing the love of Christ day after day with their message of hope. A message that proved again and again to be the aroma of life to many, but, sadly, the stench of death to some.

FREE FOR NOW

So they called them and charged them not to speak or teach at all in the name of Jesus. But Peter and John answered them, "Whether it is right in the sight of God to listen to you rather than to God, you must judge, for we cannot but speak of what we have seen and heard."
(Acts 4:18–20)

"Hey you!" A police officer grabbed Mike by the shoulder as he sat surrounded by a group at the Monkey Place one evening. It had been only six weeks since the ministry began and the evening question-and-answer period had become a regular part of his schedule. "You are coming with us!" the police demanded.

WHAT TO TEAR DOWN NEXT

In 1987, Ronald Reagan gave one of his most famous speeches during his presidency. He stood before the Berlin Wall with 45,000 in attendance and said, "General Secretary Gorbachev, if you seek peace, if you seek prosperity for the Soviet Union and Eastern Europe, if you seek liberalization: Come here to this gate! Mr. Gorbachev, open this gate! Mr. Gorbachev, tear down this wall!"[1]

In eighteen months that wall was "torn down," and the hope of something better emerged in the hearts of people. What that meant for most was that their lives would be better economically.

And in some ways, life in Eastern Europe has gotten better over the past twenty-five years, but not every change has been good. Especially for the older generation, life has become much more uncertain. Pensions have dwindled far below what is possible to live on. Medications for the terminally ill have become harder to obtain.

Democracy promised the hope of a better life, but for many that hope faded into disillusionment. And today people struggle to understand what went wrong. What else needs to be "torn down" in order to make life better?

In the midst of this, resentment toward westerners grew, in some cases with good reason. Too many foreigners arrogantly came to Eastern Europe acting like they had the answers for these "poor, sad people." And yes, some were missionaries.

---

[1] http://usgovinfo.about.com/od/historicdocuments/a/teardownwall.htm

But the gospel is not a cheap Western idea. It is not linked to democracy, a free market or healthcare. The gospel is the power of God unto salvation. God is saving people in hellholes all over the world. Places where governments rule with an iron fist, where healthcare is nonexistent, and where basic human rights are ignored. And at the same time, God is saving people in the affluent countries of the West.

It is a reality that most western missionaries are wealthier than the people they go to serve. Therefore, it is critical that missionaries be very clear that their message is not an American one. The hope of the nations is not America and its present prosperity. Our hope is Jesus. As missionaries, we can love our own country and love our adopted one as well, but nothing compares to the citizenship we have in heaven. We have a blood-bought passport that is priceless in comparison to our blue U.S. passport.

We are sent out to make disciples of Jesus and Him alone. It's hard to lay aside years of cultural understanding and, more than that, embrace another culture so that you can present Jesus to the best of your ability. But this is critical today more than ever.

We should not forget that Jesus is the ultimate Missionary who left the glory of heaven to come to earth. He willingly became a Man in order to save mankind. If ever there was someone who gave up everything to reach others, it is Jesus. He became one of us to reach all of us. He lived a simple life, a far cry from anything He had enjoyed in heaven. If there is anyone who could complain about the differences between His culture and the one He was sent to, it would be Jesus. No missionary has crossed so wide a gap, and yet Jesus did so with joy.

Before the young Californian knew what had happened, he and Tibor were shoved into a Serbian jail cell. What had they gotten themselves into? Were they really to be imprisoned for Christ? The two men could not help but think of how Peter and John were imprisoned often for speaking the truth in the book of Acts. Perhaps they were in good company.

Thankfully, this day's persecution would only last a few hours. The police released them with a stern warning.

"We are letting you go for now. But stop what you're doing out there." they commanded.

Walking away from the police station, the young men looked at one another soberly. They were not out to make any trouble. They did not want to be belligerent. But there was no way they could stop talking about Jesus.

Mike wondered if having a place to meet would help keep them out of trouble.

A PLACE TO MEET?

"I was wondering if you'd let us use a room in your church building?" Tibor translated Mike's words at a dozen different churches around the city. And from the stately steps of the Reformed church to the nondescript building of the Pentecostals, the answer had again and again been a resounding no.

Feeling defeated and frustrated, Mike sat down to pray. *God, I don't understand. You know we need a place. I've prayed. You know how I've prayed! But none of the these places want us.* He poured his heart out before the Father.

And as if words had been spoken from the innermost part of his soul, Mike heard, "No one pours new wine into old wineskins." The passage from Mark 2:22 echoed through his spirit. God was doing a new work, a fresh work in this part of the world, and it was happening out on the streets.

If that's how God wanted to work, then that is where they would stay until God provided something different.

ARREST ME TOO

"What are you doing here?" the secret police agent muscled in on Mike's meeting on the front steps of a downtown Catholic church. "You need to get out of here, all of you!" he yelled. Then he turned to Mike and leaned into his face. "We're going to arrest you and break this guitar over your head if you are out here tomorrow night."

Mike glanced over at his friend and translator.

Tibor was the one who had to count the cost. Mike and any other American present would just get deported after a short time in jail. But Tibor, as a citizen of Yugoslavia, had more to lose. If things went wrong, he faced a prison record that could tarnish the rest of his life.

Tibor looked back at Mike. The Yugoslav's chest expanded with a deep breath as if he were preparing to take a plunge into deep waters. Mike wondered what he was thinking. Then he saw it—a glimmer beaming from his eyes. Tibor's countenance shone with an inexplicable confidence as he turned to the police officer and lifted his arms, wrists together, and said, "Arrest me now!"

Mike jumped up beside Tibor facing the police officer. "Arrest me too!" he cried.

Agitated, the secret policeman shuffled awkwardly. "If you guys are out here tomorrow night then you will regret it."

"But what are you going to do with all these people?"

Mike and Tibor

Mike pointed to the crowd who came to hear the message. "Are you going to arrest them, too?"

The policeman sighed, clearly irritated with the situation. He reiterated his threat and walked away.

As if reliving the book of Acts, Mike, Tibor, and the new Christians of Subotica faced the same dilemma Peter and John underwent in the days of old, when the chief priests demanded they no longer preach Jesus.

Although brave in the face of threats, Tibor and Mike headed home with a deep sense of trepidation hanging over them. It was more than being sent to prison. Concern brimmed in their hearts for the new believers. Was anybody ready for what could happen?

CRISIS POINT

The following night the young men went out to preach, share, and teach like they had so many nights before. Although the sun slipped behind the gray buildings and the evening grew cool like any other night, it was not any other night. Tonight the tension and, yes, even fear, grew so dense you could almost cut it.

Mike, Tibor, and the other leaders huddled together on the street and began to pray. As that street corner gave way to the throne room of God, they found themselves imbued with a supernatural courage. After the last "amen," the young evangelists gazed into each other's eyes with a renewed determination. Mike responded, "Let's go for it."

Outside in the park, as Mike began strumming his guitar, he could not help but scan the crowd for the threatening men in uniforms. But in time, he lost himself in worship. They sang, prayed, and preached as they always did. Nothing seemed different.

Then in the darkness, in the back of the crowd, he saw a glimmer from the uniform cap. The police had come, just as they promised. Mike kept teaching, and Tibor kept translating. The officers had not made their move yet, so the young Californian would keep speaking until they forced him to stop.

"You live in a city called Subotica, the city of freedom," Mike preached. "But true freedom is not found in a city. It is not found in any political system old or new. True freedom can only be found in Jesus Christ." Mike proceeded to explain the the gospel of grace with clarity and precision.

The two policemen meandered at the back of the crowd, but they did not rush up to shut down the gathering. In fact, they seemed to be listening. Their interest piqued as Mike began his question-and-answer time. They pressed in closer to hear more. By the end of the night many more souls had come into the kingdom, two of which wore the uniform of the Yugoslav police.

THE COMING STORM

While heaven celebrated the countless new believers in Subotica, the dark clouds of war drew closer on the horizon. Fear and paranoia rose to new heights as Yugoslavia began to fall apart. During the summer of 1991, Slovenia broke away to become an independent state in its Ten-Day War. Croatia wanted to follow suit, but its road to independence would prove to be a longer, bloodier journey.

An American in the midst of such unrest could not help but spark suspicion. Mike continued to preach and teach the Bible despite the political turmoil. And God continued to work, drawing many of the city's youth to Himself. But these new believers came from families where issues of faith were taboo at best. As political tensions increased, police began going to their homes and warning parents that their kids were consorting with a suspected American spy. In turn, the parents would forbid their kids from seeing Mike and seeking God.

SUBVERSIVE WORK

The Son of Man has come eating and drinking, and you say, "Look at Him! A glutton and a drunkard, a friend of tax collectors and sinners!" (Luke 7:34)

"Bang! Bang!" Mike heard a frantic knock at the door at eleven o'clock that night. He opened the door and found a teenaged girl standing there. She used to come regularly to the gatherings.

"My parents don't want me coming anymore," she explained. "They burned the Bible you gave me." Mike and Tibor sat with her as she told how her parents had grounded her for three months. "But I had to sneak out and come see you tonight because I need six Bibles for my friends at school. I shared the Lord with them."

Even in the face of paranoia and persecution, the gospel of grace was spreading.

"I wish I could still come to the meetings," she said sadly. "But my parents won't let me go out at night."

"Why don't we pick you up after school in our car?" Mike thought aloud. "We can do a little Bible study so you can keep learning."

"Yeah, then we'll just drop you off down the street," Tibor added. "No one will ever know."

And so it began. The "subversive" work. It was not the work of a CIA agent that the government suspected Mike of being. He would subvert the works of darkness by smuggling Bibles to anyone willing to read them. He would teach anyone willing to listen.

The kids responded with devotion to the Lord even in the midst of persecution. Teens would hide beneath their blankets late in the night studying their contraband Bibles with flashlights.

A MEETING PLACE

In the fall of 1991, barely a year into ministry, the church of the streets found a home, one as unconventional as the church itself. Where a church would normally have stained glass windows, this place only provided broken panes. Where a church would have angelic arches, the building boasted broken beams. Dilapidated and deteriorating, the old house was a lot like all who had come to grace. As they investigated the structure further, they discovered it had no foundations at all. It probably should have just been condemned and demolished, but instead God saw fit to redeem it for His own purposes.

After the most essential renovations were complete, Mike stood before this unique congregation attempting to express words of appreciation as he dedicated the building to God's service. As he opened his mouth to speak, his voice failed him. A swell of emotion caught in his throat, and tears welled up in his eyes. Mike was speechless. All he could do was cry. For although Yugoslavia was falling apart, God was still so good. This was proof.

Taiwo working on renovations of Calvary Chapel Subotica

Mike tried to compose himself. But he just couldn't. No words were said. Perhaps no words needed to be said. The congregation broke into songs of praise and that was enough. Praising God said it all.

WHAT IS A CHURCH?

Many churches in America start in someone's garage or living room. Life Church in Oklahoma City, which is today one of the largest churches in America, began in 1996 in a two-car garage. As a church grows it might move into a strip mall or rent a school for Sunday services. In 1985, Calvary Chapel Fort Lauderdale began their services in a funeral home with only a few in attendance. Today their weekly attendance has expanded to more than 20,000 people.

If God allows, as a church continues to grow, they might one day be able to buy their own property. Chances are it will not look anything like the churches of old with their steeples and stained glass windows. In America, this is common, but it's not so normal in Europe.

The church in Europe has existed since the Apostle Paul came to Greece in approximately AD 51. In fact, there were Christian communities in Hungary by the 3rd century. One of the earliest translations of the Bible outside of the traditional Latin was into Hungarian (1420–1430). So it is clear that a form of Christianity has been woven into the history of this land. Sometimes that form was good and other times it was not. Regardless, it has impacted the people's cultural view of what a church is supposed to be.

"That's not a real church," people have been known to say when they first arrive at a Golgota service in Hungary. Most of the congregations rent rooms in a convenient location. Few own their buildings and none fulfill the historic European idea of steeples and stained glass. The very fact that our churches do not look like "churches" has definitely turned some people off and perhaps even driven them away.

But we believe the church is not a building; it is the people of God gathered under the name of Jesus. The Church is the redeemed worshipping the Redeemer.

In the New Testament, Paul greeted the churches that met in the various homes of the leaders. So in reality, the Golgota church building predates the grand buildings of the Middle Ages. We have gone all the way back to the 1st century model: homes, parks—wherever we can gather to worship the Lord.

CHANGE

"According to the grace of God given to me, like a skilled master builder I laid a foundation, and someone else is building upon it. Let each one take care how he builds upon it. For no one can lay a foundation other than that which is laid, which is Jesus Christ." (1 Corinthians 3:10–11)

A real church with a real building—God was breathing change into the life of this congregation in Subotica. From the time services started in that rickety old place, the season of the streets had come to a close, and God began a period of taking His new believers deeper.

As Mike's time in Subotica came to an end, he came across the same man who had lambasted him long ago for being a rich American who could not understand.

"You know us now because you've lived here," the man said humbly as he looked deep into Mike's eyes. "You've gone through the trenches."

Mike thought back over all he had come through since first getting off that plane in Belgrade two years before. The truth was that he loved Yugoslavia. He truly loved these people. They had become a part of him. This God-instilled love shone so clearly that it could melt even the cold heart of this harsh critic. And on that night, the critic of days past was transformed into a brother for eternity.

6

IN THE
TRENCHES

By November 1991, Yugoslavia was crumbling into all-out civil war, leaving a trail of terror as massacres and mass graves swept through the breakaway Republic of Croatia. The church in Subotica was an oasis of stability in the midst of turmoil. While Hungary had been spared the bloody barrage of war in the post-communist era, spiritual darkness there waged a ruthless campaign against God's work and His people.

GODFORSAKEN PLACE

"I believe; help my unbelief!" (Mark 9:24b)

Ugly gray buildings shot up on both sides of Paul Lange as he walked toward the small apartment that housed the Calvary Chapel missionaries in Baja, Hungary. The bent and broken awnings filled with mud played host to ratty bushes that grew through the cracks. The filth of the city's unrestrained pollution seemed to cling to everything. Paul shook his head and said to himself, *Who can live in such a place?*

Perhaps God smiled from the heavens at that moment, as this forlorn city would become Paul's home for the next five and a half years.

The scenery served an appropriate landscape for the spiritual atmosphere. Named "Baja," which translates "trouble" or "difficulty," the city's symbol included an image of the Fall of Man: Adam and Eve taking of the fruit, while the devil looks on in glee.

Just as Satan pried a wedge between God and man on that fateful day so long ago, the church in Baja suffered severe divisiveness from early on. The first six months of ministry in the city seemed to be an explosion of faith that mirrored God's movement in Subotica. Then things began to fall apart. Misunderstandings collided with misplaced expectations. The result was a church atmosphere awash in suspicion, doubt, and distrust.

With these rumblings bubbling just below the surface, Rod struggled to maintain peace, but when reinforcements arrived, the nondescript tensions became tangible.

"Tell the new missionaries they should go home," a translator told Rod as Paul and his wife Jeanette arrived to support the ministry. "We don't want them here!"

The antagonism came as no surprise to Rod. He had known things had been going awry for some time. But for the new missionary couple, such a bitter welcome to missionary life was like a punch in the gut.

FOUNDATIONAL FRIENDSHIP

Missionary life can be tough, and those training to enter the mission field hear that a lot before they go. But how those difficulties will manifest is hard to predict. Many missionaries show up in a new land with a certain level of expectation only to discover they cannot even go to the store without feeling like idiots. Besides the cultural adjustments, the utter rejection from the people they long to serve can make it hard for a missionary to find a reason to stay. So what keeps missionaries at their posts? A commitment to God and His calling is a big part of it.

Paul, Greg, and Rod

Beyond that God often uses friendships to sustain His people through the direst of circumstances.

Rod Thompson and Paul Lange's friendship had developed long before either of them considered serving together in Hungary. Prior to the mission field, the two worked in plumbing together and were a part of the same home fellowship back in California. That friendship would help them to weather many storms.

UNWANTED, YET CALLED

For the gifts and the calling of God are irrevocable.
(Romans 11:29)

Unwanted by some, yet still called by God to be there, Paul and Jeanette hunkered down for a trial by fire. By this time, Greg had moved down to Subotica to lead the ministry while Mike had gone back to the States. Paul joined forces with Rod to try and make the church work, but the battle was real, spiritual, and uphill all the way. And just when he felt he might be getting a handle on things, he got news from Rod.

"Hey, I'll be going home on furlough," Rod said almost matter-of-factly one day. "So you're in charge for the next six weeks." Paul looked at his friend in disbelief, thinking, *You want me to lead when some of the folks are dead set on getting rid of me and I don't even speak the language?* He felt things could not get any worse.

HOLDING IT TOGETHER

Paul and Jeanette struggled to hold the church together while Rod was gone. They prayed constantly. Paul found himself reading through Jeremiah Chapter 1, where the prophet was called, "...to uproot and tear down, to destroy and overthrow, to build and to plant."

WRONG EXPECTATIONS

New missionaries enter a country with incredible expectations of what God is going to do. Believing that He is going to use them to transform people's lives, very few missionaries consider the fact that they must first allow God to change and transform them. In humility, they must begin by being learners of both language and customs. The missionary must understand their job is to evangelize, not Americanize. They must know the difference. In other words, the mission field is not just about a missionary going out to rescue those "poor people." Missionaries are changed in the process as they begin to discover their ideas about missions, people, and self are often incorrect. But the Lord will do a work first in the missionary.

It resonated in his heart. Perhaps this is what God wanted to do. The Lord would be rooting up, pulling down, but then there would come a time of planting and building. These were God's words of hope to him. But day-to-day life still felt pretty tragic.

Despite the couple's commitment to the church in adversity, things were not getting any better. The cracks in the church's cohesiveness, which had been all too apparent since the day of

Paul and Jeanette with their first child, Sierra

their arrival, soon gave way to crevices, and by the time Rod returned, only a thin veneer held the pieces together.

"We've got to do something about this situation," Paul told Rod during his furlough and reiterated upon his return. Rod knew his friend was right. But what should they do?

JUST UGLY

"If your brother sins against you, go and tell him his fault, between you and him alone. If he listens to you, you have gained your brother. But if he does not listen, take one or two others along with you, that every charge may be established by the evidence of two or three witnesses. If he refuses to listen to them, tell it to the church." (Matthew 18:15–17a)

Rod and Paul first attempted to privately confront those creating rifts but had no success in solving the ever-escalating problem. And so the time came to take it directly to the church, which was at that time a congregation of about seventy people.

United in heart and spirit, they stood before the congregation and read related Scripture. They then confronted the offending parties, publicly asking them to leave the church. Even as they took this harsh yet necessary steps, their hearts were aching inside. They hoped and prayed those creating fractions would leave peacefully. Maybe then the church could become healthy again.

But their hopes would not be satisfied.

The confrontation resulted in what felt like nuclear fallout. Half the people walked out of the church yelling and screaming, the other half crying. The term "church split" is a weak word to describe what happened. It was more than a split; it was a tear, a rip, a slash job that left the already wounded congregation in tatters.

STARTING OVER

Heartbroken over the dismal situation, Rod, Paul, and Jeanette began to pick up the pieces. They were left with a congregation of about twenty-five people. Then a need arose in Subotica. The Subotica church needed someone to oversee both the ministry and the renovations of their new church building, a trying and tricky task in a nation being torn apart by civil war. With his knack for building along with his skills as a plumber, Rod proved to be the best guy for the job. But of course, that left Paul and Jeanette behind to clean up the mess.

For Paul, Hungary was just hard. Granted, he had entered the ministry at a less than ideal time. He had come through that horrible shattering of a congregation. But in truth, it was more than that. He watched as his Swedish wife moved so naturally in the ebb and flow of the Hungarian life and culture. Jeanette was learning the language and connecting with the people in deep and genuine ways. Paul felt like he was not. He felt trapped in culture shock and unable to escape it.

He did not like the aggravation of dealing with government offices, dominated by bureaucrats who seemed to enjoy making the simplest paperwork virtually impossible for anyone to obtain. He hated how irrationally hard it was

Church sign in Baja

to do the basic things of life. Worst of all, he felt utterly frustrated at his inability to speak the language, as it left him alienated from the people he longed to love and serve.

Paul remembered when Brian Brodersen had visited some time before. They had walked by a kid playing with dog poop in the street. Brian had shaken his head as he said, "You've got to be called to a place like this."

Paul nodded his head as he thought back on the comment. Brian was so right. Paul knew he was called.

"This is hard!" Paul cried out to God in his frustration. "This is not how I thought ministry would be!"

Although giving up never entered his mind, he was reaching his breaking point. Perhaps, like the church, Paul too would have to be pulled down and rooted out, before he could be built up again.

BUILDING UP

But you, beloved, building yourselves up in your most holy faith and praying in the Holy Spirit. (Jude 20)

"Buzzzzz!" The door buzzer rang at the Langes' tiny apartment in Baja.

"That's got to be him," Jeanette said to Paul, who jumped up to answer the door.

"Finally!" Paul said as he opened the door. "Rod! What took you so long?"

"I was stuck at the border for more than four hours!" Rod collapsed on the couch, totally spent. "I didn't think I'd ever get here."

Although Rod was just an hour's drive away, the war in Yugoslavia and associated embargoes made border crossings dicey. But Paul needed Rod, and Rod, the only American in Subotica, needed Paul. They needed Christian accountability. They craved the camaraderie of common culture to be able to bear the pressures of cross-cultural living in a war zone, regardless of whether the battlefield was physical or spiritual.

They would come together regularly. They would pray and sing. They would eat and laugh. Sometimes they would even sit back and watch boxing on television. Through their respective hardships, they became more than just friends. They truly became like brothers.

WORKING IT OUT

It was this bond of brotherhood that enabled them to withstand the fiery darts of the Enemy. Paul found comfort in his time with Rod. And Rod encouraged him to work through his frustration and disillusionment and discover God's lessons in it.

Although people came and went in the church, divisiveness remained a steady enemy at the gate. It was as if the church attracted trouble. One day Paul poured his heart out to God as he had done so many times before.

Lord, this is not how I thought it would be, he prayed. *Is this ministry?*

And then it came to him like a revelation. The truth was that he did not truly understand ministry. Sure, he understood the duties of pastoring and the mechanics of leading a Bible study. But somewhere along the line, he had missed the very essence of ministry. It was not about getting some experience and then moving on to something bigger and better. It was about having a heart for the people, longing for their spiritual development, and desiring what was truly best for them. It was all about truly loving them well.

God, my concepts of ministry are shallow, he prayed. *I'm so sorry.*

With a humbled heart, the young missionary begged God to help him learn to love these people. And as God began to work that love in and through him, Paul began to be able to shed his layers of discontent and exchange his own expectations for God's vision and plan, even if it proved painful at times. He was beginning to discover what true ministry was all about.

THE CHANGED AND THE UNCHANGED

Although God had changed Paul, the church's problems remained unchanged. After all, this was the church at

"Baja" meaning "trouble," and truly trouble never seemed to be in short supply. It was the kind of trouble that could, and unfortunately sometimes did, break a missionary. But it was also the kind of trouble that could take a missionary's shallow preconceptions of the Christian life and ministry and plunge him into depths he never knew existed.

DWELLING IN THE LAND

Trust in the LORD, and do good; Dwell in the land, and feed on His faithfulness. (Psalm 37:3)

We do not realize it, but most of us bring our own ideas and culture into our Christianity. We mix biblical truths with societal views and think that they are the same. For a missionary to succeed and "dwell in the land" where God has called them, they must learn to differentiate between what is biblical and what is cultural. For most missionaries this starts when they begin seeing the glaring differences between the culture they just moved to and their own. It is so easy to see the faults and inconsistencies in a new culture while being blind to one's own.

It is a major adjustment for missionaries to learn to trust the Lord by dwelling in the land God has called them to. Too often missionaries will label something "wrong" in reference to the way things work in a particular country. It is true that different cultures do things differently. But "different" does not necessarily mean "wrong."

When missionaries start saying things like, "In my country..." they are headed for trouble. Whether intended or not, these sentiments tend to build walls and alienate people. They denigrate the national Christians, making them feel like second-class citizens in the kingdom of God.

Missionaries must learn to embrace the differences, to be open to understanding different cultural perspectives, and in doing so, they may even discover some glaring inconsistencies in their own culture's spin on Christianity.

The longer the missionary "dwells in the land" (Psalm 37:3) and learns to trust the Lord to change him or her while serving others, the more joy the missionary will experience through the differences. Christianity is like a beautiful diamond that reflects the many facets of God's greatness. Our differences add to the beauty and give opportunity for "different" people to meet Jesus.

Dwelling in the land where God has called you is an important missions principle. In order to reach people we must get close to them. That means learning a new language and a new culture. That means learning to appreciate and find joy in that culture. Too many missionaries are trying to be in a foreign land but their heart is still dwelling in their homeland. This will never work. We must go to the people, just as Christ became one of us.

Being a missionary, by its very definition, requires humility and sacrifice. A missionary is simply a common person forgiven by the grace of God, learning to walk humbly before Him, with a heart and a calling to make Him known to others.

MOVING NORTH

"Do you not say, 'There are yet four months, then comes the harvest'? Look, I tell you, lift up your eyes, and see that the fields are white for harvest."
JOHN 4:35

"So why did you guys pick such a weird time to start the Bible study?" Árpi Horváth Kávai, the young translator, asked as he pointed to the clock. "I mean seriously, who starts anything at 6:15 at night?" Árpi, although originally from Subotica, had been attending the church in Szeged since coming to the city to be treated for cancer in 1993.

"No, who said that?" the young pastor, Karl Elekes, answered. "Church starts at six."

"Really?" Árpi was confused. "But I was told it starts at 6:15. That's when everyone shows up." He straightened his glasses as he explained. "And it really never gets started until 6:30. Now you're telling me that it actually starts at six."

Punctuality never took priority at Golgota. People did. And the people just loved being together. For Árpi, going through chemotherapy, the church at Szeged became a source of fellowship and encouragement, a world of faith and prayer in the midst of his crisis. It was a place where there was no shortage of friends.

Young adults and teens made up the core of all the new Golgota churches. So the majority of the church did not have to worry about children with bedtimes or other such responsibilities that would restrict their time and schedule. They were free to pursue God fully, to learn, and explore the works and will of the Lord in their world and life.

FUN IN THE SUN

The heart of man plans his way, but the LORD establishes his steps. (Proverbs 16:9)

"There's been a change," Lajos Molnár told his wife, Ági when he arrived home from work. "We'll be going to Szeged for our vacation."

Ági shook her head, trying to readjust her vacation expectations. "But I thought we were going to…"

"Like I said, there's been a change," Lajos cut her off. His workplace organized the holiday, so he did not really have a say in where they went.

Ági sighed and shrugged her shoulders. Well, at least they were going on vacation. They needed one.

As they sat down to dinner with their two daughters, Andrea and Anikó, Lajos dutifully crossed himself in typical Catholic fashion before beginning the meal. Ági rolled her eyes, annoyed by her husband's devout Catholicism. She had no interest in religion. In fact, it kind of offended her.

The family traveled from their home in Csolnok, near the historic city of Esztergom in northern Hungary down south to Szeged. When they arrived at their hotel, they discovered it swarming with foreigners—an outreach team from America. Intrigued by what could bring a bunch of Americans to a Hungarian college town in midsummer, Ági and Lajos began asking questions. They were surprised when they were invited to take part in their events, but they attended every evening session.

After the outreach concluded, the group of Americans gathered in the lobby to load up their van, and the Molnár family rushed in to say goodbye.

Ági, previously so stone cold regarding issues of faith, stood with tears streaming down her face. "We asked Jesus into our hearts last night!" she announced. "Lajos and Andrea too!"

They never dreamed that the change in their vacation destination could lead to such a transformation of their lives and relationships. When they returned to their home they sought out a church family, but did not have any luck. They wrote letters to Szeged and Baja, begging for missionaries to come plant a church in their area.

MOVING NORTH

And Jesus went throughout all the cities and villages, teaching in their synagogues and proclaiming the gospel of the kingdom and healing every disease and every affliction. (Matthew 9:35)

Answering this desperate plea, a young Hungarian woman named Ildi Bacskó, who had come to Christ in the early days of Mike Harris' ministry in Subotica, along with four guys from California, answered the call to help the Molnár family reach their community for Christ.

Upon the Californians' arrival, Ildi could not help but smirk as she discovered the guys' culturally clueless expectations of what life in Hungary would be like. Their ideas ranged from images of the Asian jungles to that of a Siberian wasteland. She suspected they were pleasantly surprised to find themselves in a cozy, although crowded, Hungarian home. The Molnár family hosted the team for the first three weeks, and they held regular Bible studies in their home for all their friends and neighbors.

The group soon settled in the nearby city of Esztergom, initiating outreaches in the city while still maintaining the village Bible study in Csolnok.

RUSSIA TO HUNGARY

And that's when I entered the picture. In 1992, I spent the last few months of high school praying with my friends about doing missions work. We all sensed that it was a unique time in human history. The Iron Curtain had fallen. The Berlin Wall had crumbled. Our nation's archenemy, which we had called the "Evil Empire" for so long, had fallen and now had opened its borders to missionaries. Russia seemed like the appropriate place for us.

Moscow was unlike any city I had ever visited—opposite from Orange County, California in every way. I traded shopping malls for breadlines, and bike rides along the beach for skateboarding in Lenin Square. Ministering in a land not so different from the Wild West, I discovered a world where organized crime pulled all the strings and, strange as it seems, the Mafia were the ones to make friends with because you did not know whom to trust. It was sheer craziness, a "fly by the seat of your pants" sort of life and ministry where anything could happen at any moment and often did. Honestly, I enjoyed my experience there because it taught me that every crisis was simply an opportunity for God to work.

While in Russia, I experienced a myriad of emotions. I vacillated from excitement to fear to extreme loneliness at times, but I believed God had called me there to share the gospel. After six months I was back in California waiting for the next step. Although short-lived, my time in Russia ignited a passion for missions that continued to grow. One day I met up with Greg Opean, an old friend who was on a visit back from Hungary. He and I began sharing stories about our experiences. More than anything, I wanted to return to Russia, but my visa had been denied.

"Dude, why don't you come to Hungary?" Greg suggested.

"Hungary?" I responded. "But I want to go back to Russia."

"Who knows? Maybe God will open the door for you to get to Russia from there," he explained. "And in the meantime, there's lots you can do in Hungary."

It seemed as good an idea as any, so in 1993 I prepared to move to Esztergom, Hungary to help out with the new church plant Greg was leading.

NEW MISSIONARY IN TOWN

A 19-year-old kid ready to conquer the world, I wandered through the Budapest train station in the wee hours of the morning. I was jet lagged from the ten-hour flight from Los Angeles to Munich, compounded by the fourteen-hour train ride to Budapest. Through my exhaustion, I searched the station for my brother, PJ Metzger, who was spending the summer serving in Hungary, and my friend, Mike Montgomery, who had promised to meet me. But the sparsely populated train station left little doubt that they were not there. It was two in the morning, and I was lost in a country where I did not speak the language.

Granted, it was not my first time troubleshooting awkward situations on the mission field. I thought back to my time in Russia where life always proved unpredictable. And here I found myself again in one of those crazy situations.

The old train station reeked of smoke and urine. It reminded me of Russia, and that was oddly comforting. I gazed up to see an old woman walking through the station. I was sure she did not speak English, so I approached her with the only other language I knew on any level, Russian.

Thankfully, she knew a great deal of Russian, but not by choice. Forty years of Soviet domination had left a generation Russian literate, but equally Russian adverse. Forced to study the language of their oppressors, the Cyrillic letters and Slavic sounds came with plenty of baggage. I would soon learn that my Russian language skills served to reopen old wounds in Hungary.

HIT THE GROUND RUNNING

I quickly discovered I had gotten off at the wrong train station. Who knew Budapest had multiple stations? The confusion and chaos of my night dawned into a much more promising morning as I finally caught up with my brother and Mike, and together we made our way to Esztergom, located north of Budapest on the Slovak border.

It beamed with all the charm expected of a European city, from classic old buildings to its picturesque walking street. But I was too tired to appreciate it. When we finally made it to the small apartment. I crashed and did not wake up for hours.

"We've got a Bible study, so I hope you are rested enough." PJ told me when I finally got up. I struggled to get my bearings as I began to realize I was now living in a tiny two-bedroom apartment (three rooms total) with four other guys. If that was not crowded enough, the place played host to the bi-weekly Bible studies.

Within the hour, the place brimmed with around thirty young people eager to study the Word of God. The quality of friendship and fellowship was so full of the Lord's grace that it made me feel instantly welcome and a part of this incredible work of God.

Greg Opean had become a pioneer in church planting for Golgota. After serving in Baja and Subotica, he now led the effort in Esztergom, and he quickly became a very close friend to me. Greg would be teaching that night in his casual, seemingly off-the-cuff style, which made the environment all the more comfortable, perhaps too comfortable.

A LITTLE TOO COMFORTABLE

The night was hot, and the crowded apartment provided little air circulation. Still reeling from all the travel, I struggled to keep my eyes open as Greg began to teach. I remember sitting on the floor and trying to prop my head up against a bookcase, so I would look like I was awake. Then I felt my mind slip into sleep. I jerked myself subtly and dragged myself back into the world of the living. But my efforts to avoid slipping into slumber were short-lived. I again reached for the bookcase to try and pull myself back, but there was no fighting it. I was dead asleep.

An uproar of laughter suddenly woke me up. I looked around wondering what was so funny only to discover that I was the butt of the joke. In my fuzziness, I had reached out, not to the bookcase, but to the young woman sitting beside me and fallen into a deep sleep with my head on her shoulder. My first day in Hungary, and in my altered state of consciousness, it looked like I was already hitting on the girls of Golgota Esztergom!

GIRLS OF ESZTERGOM

And there were many girls in Esztergom. When the church reached fifty or so people, forty-five were female. And so some began to joke that instead of "Calvary Chapel Esztergom," the name should be "Calvary Chapel Estrogen." Unfortunately, the lopsided demographic also led to some dark accusations. Some people in the city rumored that the church was just a front for drug dealers and a prostitution ring.

Angry and hurt, it would have been easy for us to "grow weary in well doing." But we had to realize that this kind of attack was nothing new. In the book of Acts, Paul often had to the deal with bands of people, even civic leaders, who spread lies to try and destroy his credibility and end the work of God. God stood greater than all the wickedness and deceit, and it was our job to keep teaching God's Word, loving people, and pointing them to Jesus.

ENTICING DISTRACTIONS

"Open your Bibles to the book of John," Greg said as he began to teach the Word one afternoon. The sun shone bright, and the weather had been so good lately that we started meeting at the park for the studies. The park proved to be a great venue because not only could we enjoy the sun, we also attracted new people who just happened to pass by and were curious about faith.

Greg began teaching as the small congregation listened. About half way into the teaching, he began to notice that while all the women of the congregation seemed to be paying close attention, all of us guys were staring down at our Bibles. Not a single one of us would look at him as he taught. In fact, we would not look anywhere. Our eyes were locked on our Bibles.

Feeling a little awkward, Greg managed to finish the teaching and wrap up the study. The first chance he got, he confronted us.

"What was wrong with you guys today?" he asked. "Why wouldn't you look at me?"

We all looked at each other uncomfortably. "So I guess you never saw it?" someone said.

"Dude! What are you talking about?" he asked impatiently.

"There was a woman sunbathing topless right behind you!" we explained.

REALIZING WHAT'S AT RISK

As a band of young, red-blooded American men, we quickly discovered two things:

1. Hungarian women were beautiful.

2. Modesty, at least in the way we defined the word, did not exist in Hungary!

Of course, it was not that Hungary had absolutely no sense of modesty. It's just that forty years of communism, which tried to eradicate God from society, left people with virtually no moral compass. For us single guys, temptations loomed everywhere, and the issues of accountability and living above reproach were very real. Greg took the lead in creating an atmosphere of openness and honesty. He knew we had to talk about our struggles and pray about them together if we were to conquer them. He encouraged us to share what was in our hearts and not allow our thoughts to get out of control.

If there were any doubts in our minds, our sending pastor, Chuck Smith of Calvary Chapel Costa Mesa, made it crystal clear what the consequences of failing in this area would be.

"Let me put it to you this way, guys," he told us directly when we shared our struggles with him. "If you fall into sin, it's over. You will be flipping burgers back in America." If we could not control our own desires, we would probably be done in the ministry. We would forfeit the privilege of being a part of all this. The stakes were high.

SKATEBOARDING FOR CHRIST

It was a great day when God began adding guys to the church, starting with an unlikely teenager.

My brother, PJ, and Matt Coyne were both avid skateboarders always looking for a place to skate. One day they stumbled upon a gangly teenager riding around on his board in Esztergom.

"Szia!" PJ greeted him. "Hey, do you know where there's a good place to skate?"

The teenager looked at them confused. Clearly, he did not speak English. Thankfully, a passerby stopped to helped. The kid's name was Jani Németh, and he invited them to a party that night where a lot of skaters would be hanging out.

"Cool!" they said and then parted ways. Jani probably thought he would never see them again, but that night they showed up at the party. By the time they arrived, Jani was completely stoned. Despite the fog that clouded his brain, he agreed to meet them the following day.

Hungarian-English dictionary in hand, PJ and Matt shared the gospel with Jani. And the words of life piqued the teen's interest because he was truly in need of hope. Having lost his father when he was quite young, Jani Németh was raised by his mom under extremely difficult circumstances. From the seventh grade he started drinking and testing out different drugs. He began skateboarding with his friends, but at one point all his friends suddenly ditched him. Jani's damaged identity was shattered further and he was left alone. But at this broken time, he found himself surrounded by these foreigners who were telling him that God loved him.

"Do you want to come to a Bible study tomorrow?" they inquired in awkward Hungarian. Without really knowing what that meant, Jani agreed. It was at this little study that Jani experienced love without hypocrisy, grace offered by God.

Jani and these young men were inseparable from this day on. They got him a Hungarian Bible and began to read the Word together; one chapter in English and one in Hungarian. In this way, they read through all four gospels.

Jani had such a heart to be used by God and a passion for music. He learned how to play the guitar so that he could lead worship for this small fellowship, and it was not long before he was our worship leader.

A skateboarding at-risk teen had been transformed into worship leader in such a short amount of time. Only God could do this. I could not help but wonder how God would use Jani for His great purposes as he grew into adulthood.

GOOD PROBLEMS

And the Lord added to their number day by day those who were being saved. (Acts 2:47b)

Within the next few months, God continued to pour out His grace, and the church grew to seventy-five attenders. With that growth came new logistical challenges, and other setbacks were on the horizon.

"Dude! The landlord wants us out of the apartment by Friday!" Greg explained to us. That meant we had only four days to find an apartment conducive to hosting a church fellowship that grew by the day.

At this time in Hungary, such

Bible study in Esztergom

a feat would not easily be accomplished. In the days of communism, strict laws forbade any room in a home to exceed 24 square meters (260 square feet).

Oppressive officials designed the edict to prevent gatherings from occurring outside their watchful eye. As a result, finding an apartment that could double as a church meeting place proved difficult at best.

It represented a problem. But in the grand scheme of things, it was a good problem. In the past, God had proven

Himself capable and more than willing to provide everything His people needed. Why would this be any different?

Sure enough, within two days we were moving our bags into a new place that served the needs of the church better in every way.

TEACHING AND NOTES

"So Phil, you want to teach on Tuesday?" Greg asked me one morning. The Esztergom church held Bible studies three times a week and met in the park when the weather was nice. I was taken aback by the request. In Russia, I had focused my time on evangelism, not on teaching the Bible. And at 19 years old, was I really qualified to teach?

"Let no one despise you for your youth, but set the believers an example in speech, in conduct, in love, in faith, in purity." The Scripture from 1 Timothy 4:12 seemed pretty clear. In fact, that Scripture could have been the motto for all the Golgota churches cropping up in Hungary as even the "church elders" had not yet reached their thirtieth birthdays.

I agreed to try it. Feeling both honored and a bit overwhelmed, I prepared to teach my first sermon in Esztergom.

Greg, being my mentor, cast a tall shadow that was hard to live up to. Casual and conversational, Greg's relaxed style of teaching provided an example I just did not think I could imitate. I was the kind of guy who had to use notes.

I taught my first study at the park. When I looked out on the faces before me, I saw friends who were quickly becoming like family, and that made the nervousness of the moment a little easier. And so I began. By the time

I wrapped up the teaching, I felt certain I had done a disastrous job, but afterward the group responded with warmth and enthusiasm. They had been blessed by whatever words managed to work their way out of my mouth.

"You are definitely called to teach," Greg encouraged me. His words drove me to work harder and harder at teaching. I wondered if God might call me to one day pastor a church. The thought filled me with excitement and a little terror. It caused me to really seek God's call on my life.

Greg gave me the privilege of teaching more and more often, and although at first I had been a little embarrassed to use my notes, they became a part of my style and approach to teaching. After about six months, even Greg began seeing the benefits.

"Hey, I think that I should start using notes," Greg said to me as he watched me prepare for the next study.

I was learning that we all have to figure out how God is working in our lives and not try to be like somebody else. I could not be like Greg, but he was an inspiration to me. We were all growing in the grace and wisdom of the Lord, learning from God, and from each other. I felt such freedom to be myself and let God use me for who He made me to be.

IN THE SCHOOLS

For all the promises of God find their Yes in Him. That is why it is through Him that we utter our Amen to God for His glory. (2 Corinthians 1:20)

"Hey Matt, isn't that a school over there?" I asked my friend and fellow missionary one day. I had just noticed a building that had a flag out front and a plaque on the door.

"Yeah, I think so," Matt Coyne answered.

We both had the thought at the same time, "Let's go in and see if we can share!"

"We could talk to English classes!" Matt's mind raced forward. As Hungary was in a time of transition, anything could happen both inside and outside the official structures of life. We felt there was no reason not to try. The worst thing that could happen was they would say no.

But they didn't say no. The next thing we knew we were standing before a roomful of Hungarian teenagers openly sharing the grace of Jesus Christ and His salvation. Afterward, we sat down with the two English teachers. We invited them to the Bible study at the apartment that evening and both showed up.

Since the teachers spoke English, they stayed a while after the study with plenty of questions. One, who spoke better English, served as their mouthpiece. She asked why we had come to Hungary, and also about our life in America. The other woman, Magdi Radácsi, listened intently to the conversation.

The teacher who was so skilled in English faded into the crowds of Esztergom in the weeks that followed, but Magdi came back every week. Soon she surrendered her life to Christ, and God raised her up to serve as a pillar of that young church.

Magdi would attend every Bible study with her 4-year-old daughter, Lilla. They would sit on the floor in the midst of the teenagers who made up the bulk of the church. Children's ministry? It did not exist. Lilla was the only child. She just sat on the floor and listened to the study with everyone else. She never balked or complained about being bored. Little Lilla loved to worship because she genuinely loved Jesus.

One night while I was teaching I noticed Lilla writing in a notebook. It seemed strange that a 4-year-old would be writing anything. She should be coloring pictures or something.

"What are you writing there, Lilla?" I asked her in Hungarian.

"I'm taking notes on what you're teaching!" she explained.

"Really?" I was a little confused. *Was she some sort of child prodigy?* "Can I see your notes?"

She proudly lifted up her notebook showing line after line of nonsensical scribbles and pen scratches. "Wow! These are amazing notes!" I had to applaud her efforts. She grinned from ear to ear.

I could not help but wonder what a special plan God must have for this little one.

BY WAY OF BUDAPEST

By the time 1994 rolled around, a number of the kids who had come to Christ in Subotica years earlier had begun attending university in Budapest. Desiring the rich quality of Christian fellowship that they had become accustomed to at Golgota, they would make the one-hour train ride up to Esztergom every Sunday eager to hear the Word and seek the Lord. The number of these pilgrims was growing.

"Why don't you guys just send someone to start a church in Budapest?" the college students inquired. It became a serious subject of prayer. Then Greg started taking trips into Budapest to see what the Lord would do.

CULTURAL QUIRKS AND FRIENDLY PRANKS

In my first month in Esztergom, I had been given an opportunity to share the Word at a traditional church just outside the city. It was a great privilege and my friend Eddie Siladji came with me to translate.

Eddie was an ethnic Hungarian from Yugoslavia. He had served in the special forces in Yugoslavia but was disgusted by the war and wanted out. A couple missionaries agreed to try and smuggle him across the border into Hungary, which was no easy task. Miraculously, they drove up in their car and kind of bundled Eddie's paperwork in with all of their passports in the hopes that God would "blind" the guards to the reality of who Eddie was—a deserter. It worked! By God's grace Eddie made it into Hungary.

The teaching and translation had gone well during the service, and afterward the pastor invited us for lunch. We sat down and they brought out the first course—chicken foot soup. I could see the little scaly toes floating on top. I had learned enough from serving in Russia to know that when you are a guest in someone's house it is best to be thankful for what God has provided on the table and not complain. Inside I just kept staring at those feet with their little sharp toenails pointing out at me. The soup

Me and the chicken foot

turned out to be quite good, but then the pastor put a foot on a little plate next to me. I didn't know what to do so I leaned over to Eddie.

"Eddie, what am I supposed to do with this foot?" I asked.

"Oh man, it's a great honor he has given you. You have to eat it!" Eddie replied.

"How? There's no meat on it."

Eddie insisted, "You have to eat this or you will disrespect this man."

That was the last thing I wanted to do, so I just grabbed that foot and did my best to get the little bit of skin from that foot into my mouth. It did not taste great and there were all these little bones in my mouth, getting stuck between my teeth. I watched the pastor spitting them onto the plate so I just did the same thing. I looked over at Eddie who was laughing.

The pastor asked him in Hungarian what was so funny and Eddie explained that he had convinced this American that he just had to eat this chicken foot or he would offend the host. I didn't understand the words but when the pastor started laughing I caught on that I had been pranked! So much for trying to be the good missionary.

Several years later, Eddie fell in love with an American girl he met at Bible college. They were married in California, and my brother and I served as his groomsmen. At the reception, Eddie's lovely new bride was off talking with friends, and some of the people started clanging their glasses together.

As an American, I knew that this is wedding tradition for the bride and groom to kiss. Everyone there knew, except Eddie. When Eddie leaned over and asked, "What's everyone doing?" I knew I had to take this opportunity.

"Oh, this is a tradition here in America. Whenever they clang their glasses like this the groom is supposed to get up and run around the entire reception room."

"No way," Eddie said. Thankfully my brother, PJ, was there to back me up.

"Oh yeah, Eddie you gotta do it. It's tradition," PJ said.

So instead of kissing his bride, Eddie got up and literally ran right by her and continued to jog around the reception hall. People went from smiling and clanging their glasses to absolute confusion. The glasses stopped and Eddie could sense that something was "off." My brother and I were laughing so hard and he looked at us from across the room and mouthed the words, "I'm gonna kill you two!" That just made us laugh harder.

Culture is a funny thing because most of us believe our culture is the best. It becomes liberating to get outside of your own culture and learn a new one. You realize that God is a lot bigger and His love a lot wider.

BUDAPEST BEGINNINGS

"Neither is new wine put into old wineskins. If it is, the skins burst and the wine is spilled and the skins are destroyed. But new wine is put into fresh wineskins, and so both are preserved."

MATTHEW 9:17

"Hey Emő, are you coming on the hike this weekend?" Zoli Horváth asked the small-framed girl as she came down the stairs to the basement of the Hungarian Reformed church in Budapest. "Sure, I'll be there," she answered as she decided not to remove her jacket in the damp chilliness of the room. The various university students gathered chairs and arranged the room for their regular Bible study.

This weekly study had all started when Brandon Anthony, a young Canadian missionary serving with International Teams, had an idea. He went to the local Reformed church and asked to see their catechism records. While speaking with the pastor, he asked if any of the young people on this list attended church, and it turned out few actually did. Brandon asked if he could contact the youth and offer to teach a Bible study in English for those interested. The pastor agreed and the Crossroads (Keresztút) Bible study began. In the two years that followed, God had raised up a harvest of those after His own heart in the wake of crumbled communism.

The Spirit of God wove the threads of this unassuming group tightly. They shared not only Friday nights together over the Word, but also excursions and activities. They truly loved each other deeply and the fabric of their fellowship had grown rich and strong.

But now the motley group of lapsed Catholics, disenchanted Protestants, and previous pagans who was now known as Crossroads (Keresztút) found itself standing at a very real crossroad. As Brandon prepared to leave Hungary to pursue his master's degree back in Canada, he gathered the group together to talk about its future.

"So one of four things has to happen here," Brandon said. "You can find a leader among yourselves, you can invite someone in to become your leader, or everybody can find their own church," he explained. "Or you could become a church yourselves somehow."

"You know, there's this guy in Esztergom with a church called "Golgota," Szilárd Márkus suggested. He had become familiar with Greg Opean through his university friends who grew up in Subotica, and now he regularly traveled to Esztergom for church. "Some of us go up to his Bible study on Saturday each week. Maybe he would come here." Szilárd zipped up his jacket to keep warm. "Why don't some of you come to Esztergom with me and see what you think?" Szilárd suggested.

And so those traveling to Esztergom increased in number and it became clear that there might be a place for Golgota in Budapest.

BEGINNINGS

Greg stood at the door of the apartment rented by the Youth With A Mission ministry. This nondescript place, not necessarily easy to find, played host to the first Golgota Bible study in Budapest. Greg appeared a large, almost intimidating figure in the doorway

Dijana, Natalija, and Andrea

until he reached out his hand in greeting and flashed his American-style smile. Szilárd Márkus, the twins, Dijana and Natalija Grabarević, and Andrea Németh, all fruit of the Subotica ministry who were now living in Budapest, filed by and greeted Greg warmly, almost like family, because that is what he had become to them.

Others came too, including those who made up the Crossroads group. As Emő walked by, Greg greeted her like any other. But when he welcomed her something in his eyes pierced her very soul. She found it disturbing. It made her want to run away. She found a seat with the others but was overwhelmed with an intense discomfort. There was no real reason to feel so uncomfortable. And yet she did.

NOT THE PLACE I WANT TO BE!

"This isn't the place I want to be!" she said to herself and determined not to return. Emő purposely skipped the second meeting, but on the third she found herself in a quandary. There was a person she needed to meet up with who would be there. She could not seem to get out of it so she forced herself to go one more time.

Emő arrived to find the apartment brimming with people. Not only did she see friends from the Crossroads group, and the crowd from Subotica, there was a bunch of new faces she did not recognize.

"Hey Emő," Zoli called to her as she entered. "Come meet Jason Stellman, Matt Kottman, and Daniel Carter." Zoli ushered the girl over to the group. "These guys just arrived from America!"

As the guitars began to strum and people began to sing, a spirit of sweet worship descended. Emő sat back and looked at the Americans, worshiping through their jet-lagged reddened eyes. *These guys sat on a plane for countless hours just to come here where everything is so hard for them, in a different country with a different language and culture—just because they want to tell us that Jesus loves us,* she thought to herself.

Emő shook her head, perplexed. It was all so shocking and incomprehensible, and just as disturbing as the way

Greg had looked at her when he greeted her at that first meeting. And yet it was all so much like Jesus. Could it be that it was "Jesus in them" that rattled her soul?

She knew they would ask for people to come help with the outreach, to translate and equip the Americans for effective ministry in Hungary. As hard as she had tried to avoid these people, she now found herself strangely drawn to them. Fluent in English, she was well suited to serve, and after the Bible study, she found herself agreeing to help.

Serving as a mouthpiece for the Americans to bring a message of hope to her people impacted Emő. The petite Hungarian began to realize that God could use even her as a conduit of His power and love. And now there was no place she would rather be than Golgota.

She continued attending the Golgota Bible studies with her Crossroads friends. Coming from a high church background, the casual style of leadership and teaching continued to catch her off guard. But strange as it was, the honest way leaders shared about their own struggles and even failures somehow made faith so much more accessible than it had ever been for her before.

Others responded in like manner, and so the Crossroads group, together with college students who had migrated from Subotica, and a handful of American missionaries, ignited a small congregation that came to be called Golgota Budapest.

UNQUALIFIED TRANSLATOR

The church began to grow as teams from the States came to help with outreaches. But outreaches often did not go exactly as planned. One day as they set up for an event, the main translator rushed in, her voice cracking and failing as she tried to explain she was suffering from laryngitis. How could the team communicate the message of grace without a translator?

Then somebody got an idea. "Hey Szilárd, you will be the one translating today." Szilárd Márkus, now attending college in Budapest from Novi Sad, was involved in every possible outreach.

"I can't translate!" he reeled in fear.

"I'll help you," the scheduled translator, his longtime friend, whispered through her laryngitis. Just watch my face and read my lips.

Szilárd's hands shook as he stood up beside the speaker. Trembling he could feel the sweat building on his brow. As the American pastor began speaking, Szilárd looked down at his friend and studied her mouth.

Although his hands were shaking a bit, lipreading was something he knew he could do. A lackluster student, he had mastered the knack of lipreading to survive high school as friends would mouth the answers to exam questions during tests. Who knew God could redeem even such an illicitly gained skill?

"Szilárd, your English is so good!" Everyone congratulated him when the event came to a close. He smiled, feeling like he had served a really significant part in ministry. He was just a college kid and a relatively new Christian. And God was using him.

PUSHED FURTHER

Szilárd began feeling really confident until the same sort of thing happened again a couple of weeks later.

Szilárd Márkus

"Szilárd can translate!" Someone suggested when the scheduled translator couldn't make it. "He did a great job at the outreach!" And before he knew it, he had been shoved up front next to the speaker. But this time nobody was there to help him. He was on his own, wishing he had paid more attention in English class.

If Szilárd perspired before, this time he was sweating buckets. As the speaker began, Szilárd prayed he could get through this. He took a deep breath and opened his mouth to give a translation. And right then something just clicked. All the words, the perfect words, just flowed out of Szilárd's mind and passed through his lips. He had never been able to translate before! *How can this be happening?* he wondered. But instead of recognizing that the Spirit of God was working miracles in him, Szilárd confidently pushed out his chest. *Yeah, I am one good translator,* he applauded himself in the back of his mind.

Like magic, as the self-adulation appeared in his mind, his ability to translate disappeared. Szilárd found himself tongue tied. He could say nothing until in his heart, he acknowledged, *Oh, it was You, God! I am so sorry. Thank You, God!*

Szilárd and Ágota Márkus at their wedding with Greg on the right

At such a unique time in Christian history, God chose to raise up a new generation of believers in a new land and train them in humility and Christian service even as He used them to further His kingdom.

AT THE PARK

For by grace you have been saved through faith. And this is not your own doing; it is the gift of God, not a result of works, so that no one may boast. (Ephesians 2:8–9)

The Youth With A Mission apartment soon proved ill suited for the ever-growing group of young people. The noise level disturbed the neighbors, so Greg began searching for another place to meet. Unfortunately, nothing seemed to work out. But the weather grew warm as summer set in, so they decided to do what they had done in Esztergom—head for the park.

Nestled in the middle of the Danube River, Margaret Island serves as the city's central spot of summer splendor. Complete with fountains, rose gardens, and grassy knolls, the park was a well-suited church for the young people because Bible studies could be punctuated by picnics and sports.

As the sounds of guitar music wafted through the trees, the meetings naturally attracted curious onlookers who gathered to see what the music was all about and what this foreigner might have to say.

"Today, let's open our Bibles to the book of Ephesians," Greg said. Andrea Németh, who had come to Christ in Subotica years before, translated. In recent months, she had become Greg's primary translator in Budapest. "Let's look at what grace really means," Greg continued.

Greg's message of God's grace resounded throughout Margaret Island. The following week, more people assembled to hear his message.

"Let's open our Bibles to the book of Ephesians," Greg said the following week. "We'll start by looking at what grace really means." Andrea translated his words again. And as she continued through the sermon, she realized he was teaching the exact same message he had taught the week before. She found the redundancy irritating. But she hid her emotions and translated dutifully.

Even more people gathered the third week. The guitar strings mixed with voices of praise drawing the crowd into a view of God they had not previously considered. "Let's open our Bibles to the book of Ephesians," Greg began again. "We need to understand the meaning of grace." Andrea sighed as she translated. *You've got to be kidding!* she thought to herself, trying to hide her annoyance. *The same sermon again!* She was almost too embarrassed to translate it for the third time!

Despite what felt to Andrea like insipid repetition, more people came. People began talking, not just in Budapest but also in other parts of Hungary, about the foreigner on Margaret Island who was always talking about grace.

GRACE

"And now I commend you to God and to the word of His grace, which is able to build you up and to give you the inheritance among all those who are sanctified."
(Acts 20:32)

Grace. In a world emerging from the austere severity of communism, the message of God's grace resonated in the people's spirits. Like living water on a parched soul, the people ached for it. They understood law all too well. If they had any experience with a church, it had likely been more a religion of rules than a life full of faith and freedom. This message of grace was completely new and unconventional. Could it have really been there in the Bible all along?

"Let's open our Bibles to the book of Ephesians," Greg said yet again the fourth week. "Let's review the real meaning of grace." *Seriously?* Andrea thought to herself. *Again?! Has Greg completely lost his mind?* Andrea could not understand the point of it all. But it was not something that Greg did consciously. God just kept bringing him back to the same message each week, and each week, it seemed deeper and more real. So for him it did not feel like the same sermon. Andrea forced herself to translate a Bible study she could now almost recite word for word in her sleep.

THE WAY TO HEAVEN?

"If heaven were by merit, it would never be heaven to me, for if I were in it I should say, 'I am sure I am here by mistake; I am sure this is not my place; I have no claim to it.' But if it be of grace and not of works, then we may walk into heaven with boldness." (Charles Spurgeon)

A lot of people get caught up in the question of whether they are good enough to go to heaven. No one needs to wonder. I can answer that question. You're not even close! I'm not either. No one on this earth is good enough. That creates a really big problem if the way a person gets to heaven is through his or her own good works. Thankfully, God has provided another way, the way of grace.

God looked down and saw how badly humankind had blown it. Sin had consumed our very nature, and we stood helpless to save ourselves. Compassion filled Him and He chose to make the ultimate sacrifice to bring us back into relationship with Him. That sacrifice was the death of His Son, Jesus.

This is grace—God's unmerited favor. God, for no obvious reason, chose to give His Son to save the world from sin, that the world may know true love. God loved us not because we are so good and lovable. He loved us because He is so good and loving.

We cannot earn God's grace. If we could earn it, it would no longer be grace but works (Romans 11:6).

There is not one person in heaven who "made it" there by their own merits. We are saved because God is gracious.

In Ephesians 2:7 Paul writes, "So that in the coming ages He might show the immeasurable riches of His grace in kindness toward us in Christ Jesus." God's favor is not a one-time offer. We who have put our faith in Jesus will spend eternity learning about the kindness of God. Heaven is enthralled by the unbelievable grace of God.

CLARITY

Years later, Andrea would understand the importance of that era of redundancy on Margaret Island.

"Remember when we had to meet on Margaret Island?" Eta reminisced with Andrea. "Yes, Greg made me crazy that summer preaching the same thing over and over again." Andrea shook her head and laughed as she recalled it.

"Yes," Eta's tone grew more serious. "It was all about grace." Her eyes glazed over and the corners of her mouth turned up gently in a sober smile. "I wanted to hear it all those different times," she said. "I needed to hear it again and again to be able to understand it."

If that were true for Eta, it might well be true for countless others. Andrea grinned at her friend, awakened to the fact that even in this thing that seemed so ridiculous and irritating at the time, God was showing His grace.

READY FOR GRACE

The message of God's grace has brought so much joy and freedom to many in Eastern Europe. This is a region of the world that, for decades, only knew the oppression severe laws wrought on all aspects of life. But Soviet dominance extended far beyond laws and governance into the very psyche of the people.

Hungarians courageously fought Soviet dominance in 1956, but it was a short-lived revolt. The people rose up against domination, but the Soviet Union lashed back with violent aggression. Being controlled became more than a reality; it became a national identity. Communism was not the only contributor. Hungary's history is a long litany of failed revolutions giving way to a pessimistic national perspective.

And with this pessimistic view comes a deep-rooted belief that they are no good. While this is a drastic over-simplification, it illustrates why I believe the doctrine of grace is such a powerful force in Hungary today.

In America, we are often told in church not to think so highly of ourselves. To oversimplify Americans, we are a "take it" kind of people. We came to a new land, conquered that land, fought others from trying to control us in that land, and succeeded. We see ourselves as winners.

This can be a stumbling block for Americans as we must come to understand our own unworthiness before we can embrace God's grace.

The Hungarian mentality of pessimism and defeat has allowed them to understand all too clearly how hard it is to live up to the law. Instead of expecting or demanding God's accolades, they tend to wonder, *Could God really forgive me? Does God really love me?*

And that is when God's grace shines into the darkest places, answering, *Yes! He loves you not because of who you are but because of who He is!* This truth of God's unmerited kindness is changing a nation.

Today, the culture in Hungary is changing and many of those past ideas of national identity are changing with it. But grace is still grace, and it is the sweetest sound to the hopeless and to the hurting.

THE NOMADIC CHURCH

"For as the heavens are higher than the earth, so are My ways higher than your ways and My thoughts than your thoughts." (Isaiah 55:9)

The church moved from Margaret Island to a beautiful room up on Castle Hill. But when rent skyrocketed from around $40 to $200, it was time to move again. Meanwhile, the little group of ten to fifteen had grown to forty or fifty. After renting several different places on the Pest side of the city, this nomadic church's numbers were surpassing 100 and nearing 200.

While renting a room at the Social Democratic Party headquarters, the set up crew arrived early one morning to find the doors locked. Church leaders soon discovered the owners had decided they no longer wanted to rent out the room. No notice. Nothing. They were just met with locked doors on a Sunday morning.

Where could they go?

"Well, we could always go back to Margaret Island," someone suggested in the midst of the panic, remembering the church's recent history. So they hung signs and placed ushers to redirect everyone coming to church. And once again, Golgota Budapest became the church on the island.

When winter came, the church moved into yet another building.

Over six years, the church moved twelve times. In the natural world, such a period of wandering could be the death of an organization. But something supernatural was at work—as supernatural as grace itself. In the spirit of the Crossroads group and other Golgota congregations, the church was rooted not in times and places, but in relationships. The friendships wove together a strong tapestry, sealed by the ultimate relationship with the Father through the Son. So although these were the days before websites and instant messaging, people still managed to get the message of the latest church move. And instead of dwindling numbers, the congregation just kept growing.

Most Hungarians consider themselves Christian. The large majority associate themselves with the Catholic church. The second largest Christian group in Hungary is the Hungarian Reformed church, which traces its history back to the Protestant Reformation.

SETTING DOWN ROOTS

Pray without ceasing.
1 THESSALONIANS 5:17

"Whatever you ask in My name, this I will do, that the Father may be glorified in the Son."
JOHN 14:13

"Ask, and it will be given to you; seek, and you will find; knock, and it will be opened to you."
MATTHEW 7:7

"Lord, look, the oil company has it's own building," Rob Verdeyen prayed as he glanced up at the OMV gas station in Budapest. "But Your people don't have their own place." Rob's fingers scratched his sandy-colored hair as his eyes continued to dart around the streets. "Lord, the McDonald's over there has its own building, but Your people, Golgota Budapest, do not have a place to call their own." His head then bowed and eyelids pressed together tensely. "Please, Lord, give them their own building."

Greg had known Rob for many years, since Rob served as a high school pastor in Costa Mesa, California. Now as the pastor of Calvary Chapel Corvallis, Oregon, Rob had become a supporter, prayer warrior, and encourager of God's work in Hungary. The fact that his wife, Susie, was the daughter of Hungarian immigrants further cemented his love and commitment to this part of the world.

Greg prayed alongside Rob as they drove through the city. He was struck by his friend's passion about this. Sure, the idea of having a building had occurred to him before, but to tell the truth, he had not put too much thought or prayer into it. It had never been a priority. But this little prayer-saturated car ride sparked a vision in his spirit. *Could God really want to give Golgota Budapest a building?*

After Rob had returned to Oregon, his prayer stayed with Greg. Greg shared it with his new bride, Jennifer, and the other leaders in the church. Soon they found themselves praying Rob's prayer each time they met. Spiritual ground was already breaking, though nobody knew where or when God would provide the physical structure.

CHAPTER 9

A CHARMING THEATER

But, as it is written, "What no eye has seen, nor ear heard, nor the heart of man imagined, what God has prepared for those who love Him." (1 Corinthians 2:9)

"We found this theater on the edge of the city," Greg explained to his new in-laws, Ed and Raelynn Rea, during their yearly ministry trip to Budapest. "This could be the facility that God wants to provide for us. It's just so charming. I think you'll love it."

Ed and Raelynn had a history in Hungary. In the 1970s, they had toured behind the Iron Curtain as musicians turned Bible smugglers with their toddler Jennifer. Now, with their daughter and son-in-law, they were looking at buildings for the church.

They pulled up to a lovely structure and got out of the car. Greg and Jennifer eagerly showed her parents around and talked about all that they could do with such a place.

"It's really nice, Greg. How many people does this place seat?" Raelynn asked as her mind started to calculate.

"One hundred fifty people," Greg answered quickly. He had already thought it all out.

Raelynn shook her head. "Greg, I think it's way too small. The Lord is doing something much bigger."

Greg sighed. *Bigger?* he thought to himself. A building of this size on the edge of the city would sell for close to $200,000. That was two hundred grand he did not have. And his mother-in-law thought he should go bigger? It was crazy.

The truth, although he might not have said it out loud at the time, was that he did not have faith for bigger.

Szilárd, that university kid who had used his school-cheating skills to translate for an outreach years before, had become Greg's righthand man in ministry in Budapest. Greg was ready to move forward on the building, so he asked Szilárd to contact the seller.

In the meantime, Greg had to figure out how to raise the money to make an offer. Many churches had come through Budapest to minister with short-term teams. They had helped in the outreaches that had contributed to building the congregation. They had been touched and moved by the hand of God through the ministry in Hungary and had stated, "If you ever need money for special projects with the church, let us know."

He contacted about ten different churches with the request. They responded, enabling Golgota Budapest to make an offer of $150,000 for the small, old theater.

Greg smiled at Szilárd after he hung up the phone making the offer. "This is it," he said brimming with excitement in the expectation that God really might be doing this. God might really give this nomadic congregation a home of its own.

Days passed. No response.

Weeks passed. Still nothing.

"Contact them again and tell them we are willing to pay full price," Greg told Szilárd. The desire to give the church a place of its own now burned deeply in his soul.

Even at full price the company would not respond to the offer.

"What's wrong with these people?" Greg vented aloud one day. "It's like they don't want to sell the building."

"Yeah, I think that's exactly it," Szilárd responded.

"What do you mean?" Greg asked.

"This company who is selling the property was apparently appointed by the government to sell off all the theaters that the communists had confiscated before the change," Szilárd explained.

"So why don't they want to sell it?"

"This is the last one they have to sell." Szilárd leaned back in his chair as he shook his head. "So when this one sells, everyone is out of a job."

It was all too clear that the Lord had closed this door. At first Greg's heart ached with disappointment. He really loved that charming little theater and could imagine so much happening in that place. Then he remembered what his mother-in-law had said: "God is doing something much bigger."

Could it be true? In the midst of this crushed vision, Greg allowed God to expand his faith. He began lifting his eyes to higher horizons.

BIGGER AND BETTER

Szilárd and Greg began searching. No longer did they peruse inconvenient places on the edge of town. They were searching for a place in the heart of Budapest, in reach of the heavily trafficked ring roads that arc throughout the city.

One day they stumbled upon an old grimy, well-worn factory about 100 feet from one of the busiest intersections of the city, called Oktogon. When they walked through the site, Greg calculated how many chairs they could set up in the big room. It came out to 250!

It certainly lacked the charm of the first place, but the location was incredible. It was bigger and better. He discovered the asking price was $400,000, so he continued his fundraising campaign as Szilárd proceeded to make an offer, by faith.

The seller accepted the offer! Greg beamed with excitement. This was really finally happening! Szilárd and Greg headed over to the office to make the down payment and sign the papers. But when they arrived, the sellers informed them that they sold the building to someone else that very morning.

TWICE CRUSHED

But they who wait for the LORD shall renew their strength; they shall mount up with wings like eagles; they shall run and not be weary; they shall walk and not faint.
(Isaiah 40:31)

It was like being completely crushed a second time. Did God really want to give them a building? Was this all an exercise in futility? Feeling like the rug had been ripped out from under him, Greg found himself walking through the streets of Budapest trying to clear his heart and mind.

When he passed the McDonald's, he remembered Rob Verdeyen's prayer: "Lord, the McDonald's over there has its own building, but Your people, Golgota Budapest, do not have a place to call their own." He sighed deeply, wondering what the Lord was doing.

"Hey, Pastor Greg!" Drew Parsons, head of the Campus Crusade's *Jesus Film Project* in Russia and Europe, greeted him. Drew had been attending the Budapest church for some time, and Greg counted him as a friend.

Greg was glad to run into a friendly face. He poured his heart out to Drew right there on the street. The Campus Crusade missionary listened intently, and then thought for a moment.

"Greg, I sense that the Lord wants us to look right on one of the main boulevards," he responded. "God shut the doors because He wants us right in the heart of where the people are."

Greg reeled slightly. "Do you know how much properties on the main boulevards cost?"

Drew smiled. "Pastor Greg," he said gently. "Is anything too hard for the Lord?"

Drew said goodbye, leaving Greg there on the Budapest street. He stood silent, feeling unnaturally stretched and a bit convicted. *Here I am the pastor, the leader, and I have people in my church and in my family who have more faith than I do regarding this whole thing.*

A new heart of prayer emerged from Greg's broken spirit. As he began to walk home, he prayed, "Lord, help me to not limit You!" He shook his head as he passed the graffiti-covered walls of the downtown buildings. "I am a spiritual wimp!" he confessed to the Lord. Then he took a deep breath. "But if it is Your will, give us a place on a main boulevard."

THE PROCLAIMER

How beautiful upon the mountains are the feet of him who brings good news, who proclaims peace, who brings glad tidings of good things, who proclaims salvation, who says to Zion, "Your God reigns!" (Isaiah 52:7–NKJV)

The Proclaimer in 2001

Only days later, Greg received word that a building known as the "Híradó" was for sale. The building, another old theater, rose from the corner of a busy downtown thoroughfare, on a main tramline and almost adjacent to an underground metro stop. Perhaps more remarkable than the building's size and location was its name. "Híradó" translates as "Proclaimer."

Rich in the city's history, the property had served not only as an entertainment venue, but had featured a ticker tape during World War II. People came from all over the city to this location to learn the latest world news and critical events impacting their lives and future. *Could God want to use the Híradó to proclaim His Good News to this city?*

CONNECTING WITH THE CHOSEN PEOPLE

Szilárd called to arrange for a meeting with the owner of the Híradó, a Jewish man from Jerusalem. The man's son,

Abner (the name of King David's general in the Bible), lived in Budapest and managed their properties. Enamored with the Jewish connection, Greg found himself even more enthralled when he learned Abner had served as a helicopter pilot for the Israeli Defense Forces.

The Proclaimer today, home of Golgota Budapest

The venture of faith felt as if it were spiraling into surrealism as they sat down with Abner at the Híradó and asked the big question. "How much?"

Abner tilted his head to one side and looked at Greg and Szilárd. "We really can't let it go for much less than one million dollars."

The number fell from his lips like an anvil, crashing Greg and Szilárd back to cold, hard reality.

One million dollars. The figure reverberated into the recesses of Greg's mind. Something about that astronomical number really drove home just how out of reach all this was.

Szilárd and Greg looked at each other. "We have $400,000," Greg blurted out, as they smiled, even laughed a little at how ridiculous they must have looked.

Abner raised his eyebrows, maybe in disbelief of such a ridiculous offer. He grinned and said "Look, I can come down to $985,000, but that's all."

Greg nodded. "Abner, we have $400,000, and I understand if that sounds crazy and doesn't work for you, but that's where we are at."

Greg and Szilárd said amiable goodbyes to Abner, saddened that it did not work out. They really liked him and the Híradó seemed perfect. But at this point, it was just too far out of reach.

A NEW OFFER

Six months passed and both Greg and Szilárd made little progress finding another building to pursue. One day, when they were together, Szilárd's phone rang. Greg noticed his friend's eyes light up as he talked on the phone.

"Greg, it's Abner from the Híradó," Szilárd said after he hung up. "He wants to meet us in an hour!" Both men's imaginations soared with the possibilities. Could the Híradó be in their reach?

When they arrived, Abner wasted no time in getting to the point. "Okay guys, we have to move on this property," he said with all the intensity you would expect from an international businessman. "If you can pay $660,000, it's yours."

Greg's eyes grew big. He looked a little like a small child who had just discovered Santa came on Christmas morning. But it wasn't Santa who had smiled upon them that day. It was Jesus and His grace.

"You've got a deal!" Greg blurted out. Then realizing they did not actually have that much on hand, he added. "Give us three months escrow!"

Perhaps it was because of what he had learned in this process, but somehow Greg had faith that in three months they could have the rest of the money.

Of course, this was business, and the details had to be hashed out. Abner's father flew in from Jerusalem for the meetings, which created a unique opportunity for people of the New Covenant to intertwine ideas with those of the Old Covenant. The older Israeli man came to the meetings with his beloved Hebrew text under his arm. While lawyers worked out contract clauses, Greg capitalized on the opportunity to draw on the old man's wisdom and insight into the Scriptures. As lawyers bantered over legal jargon, clauses and conditions, Greg and the elder Israeli worked through practically every story in the Old Testament.

Greg treasured the Jewish man's insights, filing them away in his memory for use in sermons for years to come. After the last papers were signed, and the Proclaimer became the legal property of Golgota Budapest, he could not help but sense that they were all a part of some great story God was telling in modern times, a story of grace.

LEGAL TROUBLES

While owning a building allowed the church to do more than it ever had before, the new building was not all blessings. It came with a set of burdens as well.

The bell rang one afternoon at the church building. Szilárd answered it only to find the postman with some sort of official letter he had to sign for. He carefully opened the envelope and read. His eyebrows raised in abject disbelief. "We are being sued!" he said looking up at Greg.

"What?!" Greg responded.

"It's the guy who runs the convenient store," Szilárd explained. The man had a contract to rent a small room

CHURCH SUCCESS

One huge misconception in the modern church is that "big" means "successful." That is not always the case. If people are just coming out to serve as spectators at a church service, then church becomes a lot like going to a show. Participants may feel entertained, but they never really allow it to change them.

The work of grace begins on the inside. For too many people Christianity has been seen as a religion of good people trying to live good lives.

The beauty of the gospel is that God so loves the world that He gave His Son, not for good people but for all people. In a country like Hungary, where depression is such a stronghold, there is no sweeter message than God's forgiveness and love. People came to drink in the refreshment of God's grace, and their lives were transformed. They were incapable of being merely spectators in this great story of grace. Their hearts' burned with a passion to reach out to others.

While certain traits varied in the different Golgota churches across the nation, one thing remained the same: there was no separation between those being served and those serving. People got saved and saw their need to let God use them almost immediately. As a result, ministries of all kinds emerged.

for his shop out of the building at the time the church purchased it.

Unfortunately, the store was failing. The man was not paying his vendors and as time passed, he only drifted further and further in debt. When the church gave him his notice, the elders actually thought they were doing him a favor, as it would save him thousands. But apparently the man did not see things the same way. The notice had been served a few days earlier than it legally should have. Capitalizing on the innocent error, the man decided to launch an outrageous lawsuit, setting off a whirlwind of litigation that would not come to an end for another eight years.

GOOD NEIGHBORS?

"Shower, O heavens, from above, and let the clouds rain down righteousness; let the earth open, that salvation and righteousness may bear fruit; let the earth cause them both to sprout; I the LORD have created it." (Isaiah 45:8)

"We give You praises, with thanksgiving. As we lift our hands to praise You and to glorify Your name." The sound of praise permeated the main theater room of Golgota Budapest on Sunday mornings, Wednesday evenings, and sometimes for Friday night concerts. The Bible tells us to let our praise rise like incense to the Lord. Unfortunately, when the worship was going up to God it was also going up to the neighbors above; forty-six apartments, many inhabited by folks who did not appreciate the free concerts.

Fed up with the unwanted noise interrupting her life, an elderly woman set out one Friday night concert to put an end to it. She pinned her long gray strands of hair into a tight bun and marched to her broom closet. Grabbing some buckets, she promptly filled them with water. It must have been a heavy load, but one should never underestimate the strength of an old Hungarian woman on a mission. She dragged those buckets to an old grate that hung over the center of the theater. With a gleam of satisfaction in her eye, she proceeded to dump all the water she could carry into the grate and onto the pulpit below, right in the middle of the concert!

It was not the Holy Spirit that rained down that night, but an old woman's frustration!

Still, the church sought to make peace with the neighbors and serve the community in many ways. As the church grew in numbers it was also growing in maturity. This work of grace produced amazing ministries from the many grateful lives that had been touched by God.

CHRIST AND THE ARTS

The doors of the famous Híradó had opened again, and as news of it spread, many actors, singers, and musicians came to check out what was happening at the historic venue. Many gave their lives to Christ, and some even began a ministry for artists. They wrote short plays and put together groups to perform them as a way of outreach to their nation.

A country that produced such world-renowned musicians as Ferenc Liszt and Zoltán Kodály suffers no shortage of musical brilliance. And as more musicians gave their lives to Jesus, they longed to use their gifts for His glory. As a result, worship grew from a six-string guitar to an orchestra including multiple stringed instruments. One solitary missionary worship leader soon blossomed into several different groups of Hungarian musicians and worship leaders.

THE UNBORN

God moved in the hearts of others in the congregation to minister to women facing crisis pregnancies and to their unborn children. Hungary rates in the top ten nations in terms of the number of abortions performed each year. Some statistics say their are as many as 43 abortions per 100 births. In Hungarian orphanages, teens use abortion as a form of birth control—with their caregiver's encouragement and assistance. One girl, after enduring four abortions by age 15, said that she was "sick of it" and declared from then on she would no longer have relationships with boys. She hoped to find something safer in the homosexual lifestyle.

Grieving the loss of so many lives and seeing the lifelong scars that abortion leaves on women, a group within the church started a ministry called "Shout for Life," dedicated to helping those babies who have no voice. The group began to educate women who face crisis pregnancies and to assist them in finding alternatives to abortion. They offer the help and support these ladies need to get through such a difficult time.

CRAZY VISION

"Write the vision; make it plain on tablets, so he may run who reads it." (Habakkuk 2:2b)

Vision is key for missionaries and anyone who wants to be used by God. There are plenty of wonderful definitions out there to help us understand what biblical vision is. Let me add my own.

Biblical vision is seeing what God wants you to see. It is when God opens your eyes and shows you something that He sees. Vision is when Jesus said in John 4:35, "Do you not say, 'There are yet four months, then comes the harvest'? Look, I tell you, lift up your eyes, and see that the fields are white for harvest." He turned the attention to the thing that mattered most to Him; people in need of the gospel. We need to ask God to help us see what God sees.

GOSPEL CHOIR

"Wouldn't it be awesome if we had a big gospel choir?" Greg began to share his vision with his closest friends.

"Yeah, that would be cool," his friends would reply and then dismiss it as another one of Greg's crazy ideas.

The interesting thing about Greg's crazy ideas are how many of them actually came to fruition! From his vision for a building, to his vision for a radio broadcast, and even his vision for a gospel choir, they came to pass. To know Greg is to know a true visionary.

The idea of a choir seemed impossible at the time. But when God sent Mark Zeeman, an accomplished concert pianist, to Budapest, the doors began to open. Today that choir is 200 voices strong, and it has toured several countries across Europe, providing concerts and preaching the gospel message.

Golgota Budapest Gospel Choir

EXPANDING GRACE

For I am not ashamed of the gospel, for it is the power of God for salvation to everyone who believes, to the Jew first and also to the Greek.

ROMANS 1:16

Word of a new group called Golgota began to spread throughout Hungary. Keep in mind that Hungary is a small country. As of January 2014, it had a population of just less than ten million people. That means the entire country's population amounts to less than that of the county of Los Angeles. And the Christian community was even smaller, so word traveled fast. Soon it reached the college town of Debrecen, a city only fifteen miles from the Romanian border and seventy-five miles from Ukraine.

SOMEONE TO TEACH US

"Anybody want another pancake?" Bodi asked the crowd of university students who had gathered at his apartment. He glanced at his friends and their guests through his thick, round, coke-bottle glasses and smiled as he handed someone a plate of the tasty treats. The long thick braid of hair that hung to his waist seemed to exaggerate his already noteworthy height.

A medical student at the University of Debrecen, Zsolt Bodogán, known to his friends as Bodi, had come to know God the age of 17. Now they gathered regularly to combine good food for the body with a hearty meal for the soul. They represented yet another pocket of the grace God was pouring out on Eastern Europe at this unique time.

After singing and praying together, the group began talking about a new church someone had visited in Budapest—a congregation full of young people that focused on God's grace, a church known as "Golgota."

"Maybe they'd be willing to send someone here to teach us," one of the guys suggested.

"I guess we could ask," Bodi commented.

Within a couple weeks, God moved in response to their request. Christian Kingery, an American missionary, began making a regular five-hour weekly pilgrimage across Hungary from Veszprém to Debrecen to teach them the Word of God.

BIBLE STUDIES BEGIN

"Since this is our first Bible study, let's start in Romans," Christian opened his first meeting with the group. But he did not get very far. He didn't get past the first chapter or even the first verse. In fact, the whole Bible study centered on nothing but the first word: "Paul."

Bodi listened intently as Christian explained how Paul had the religious life squared away intellectually, but he never had a real relationship with God until that fateful day on the Damascus Road. Bodi's heart broke as he came face to face with the sobering reality. *Lord, I am just like Paul. I know about You on some level but I don't know You intimately or personally.* The young medical student bowed his head to hide his tears. *I don't have the kind of relationship with You that I need.*

From that moment on, Bodi could not get enough of the Word of God. He waited with bated breath for the weekly Bible studies and Christian's arrival. And he was not the only one. God was pouring out His grace on this small group of students, taking them deeper in their new faith. Finally, Bodi asked the question on everyone's mind, "So Christian, when are you going to move to Debrecen?"

It was a question that sent Christian's world into a tailspin, and within two months he had gathered his family together and relocated to eastern Hungary. Everything was moving so fast.

The new church in town, featuring an American pastor, attracted many of the city's international students. Campus Crusade missionaries also found a natural home in the church as well as a partner with a common goal of reaching the lost.

The church veritably exploded with an evangelical zeal that drew many to Christ. Bodi found himself wrapped up in the middle of it, and there was no place he would rather be. Despite the pressures of grueling medical exams in every subject from pathology to pediatrics, Bodi found his passion for God rivaling, perhaps even eclipsing, his passion for medicine. Others could see it as well.

A PROPHECY

"Hey Bodi!" One of his brothers in the faith greeted him one day. "I've got a prophecy for you!"

"Really?" Bodi listened intently, ready to test the spirits on this one. "What is it?" he asked cautiously.

"You are going to be pastor of this church someday," his friend stated emphatically.

Bodi laughed a little. "I am going to finish medical school and then go to Nepal and work with lepers or something," he explained his plans to his friend.

"Just wait and see," the fellow student pressed. "You will be pastor here."

ZEAL GONE AWRY

"For the wages of sin is death." The Scripture from Romans 6:23 could be found spray painted on buildings all over town.

"What's with the Bible graffiti?" Christian asked some of the young people in his congregation one day.

They smiled proudly and looked at each other. "We did it!" they answered.

Christian's eyebrows furrowed. He ran his hand over his bald head and said, "You're kidding? You guys know that's illegal, right?"

"It's what we're called to do!" One of the students pulled out his Bible and turned to Deuteronomy Chapter 6. "Look here it is in verse nine. It says to write God's commands on the doorposts and gates!"

Christian sighed and shook his head slightly, smiling at the young people. He appreciated their hearts for God, but clearly they had slipped off course a bit on this one.

"Guys, as Christians we need to honor the laws," Christian appealed to them gently, pointing out relevant Scripture. "We shouldn't be going around making trouble."

The zealous "artists" fully expected their pastor to commend them for their dedication. Perplexed, yet determined to continue their gospel graffiti, they grew distant and eventually left the congregation.

REFUGEE MINISTRY

"You must not mistreat or oppress foreigners in any way. Remember, you yourselves were once foreigners in the land of Egypt." (Exodus 22:21–NLT)

Many ministries emerged from this little congregation of young and new believers. Debrecen is home to one of the largest refugee camps in the country. It is one of the fundamental gateways for refugees entering Europe, so the church found no shortage of need.

Designed to serve as a refuge for people fleeing life-threatening circumstances in their own countries, these refugee camps provide only basic food and shelter. Some refugees are families seeking safety from a country torn apart by civil war. Others come from questionable backgrounds, criminals trying to avoid prosecution. This consolidation of desperate people in the worst possible situations produces an environment marked by extreme violence, alcohol, drugs, and sexual abuse. While the camp is meant to serve as a temporary home, some refugees end up staying for years as their paperwork makes its way through the appeals process.

Rosemary Kovács, the daughter of a Hungarian refugee who immigrated to the United States, returned to her father's homeland to share the gospel of Christ and led the effort to minister to the refugees in Debrecen.

The small, unassuming young woman walked the dingy halls of the refugee camp, knocking on doors and handing out Bibles in various languages. She would meet with people and try to answer their questions, and through her gentle manner and Spirit-led words, she saw people from around the world discover a Savior.

"Rosemary!" one Nigerian refugee greeted her each time she entered the little security building that served as a gate for the camp. Prince, a quiet fellow who just longed for a friend, always looked forward to visits from Rosemary and often accompanied her as she went to see the different rooms, passing out Bibles. As the weeks passed, Prince began gently answering some of the people's Bible questions, especially during the African Bible study. And

Rosemary could not help but wonder if God didn't have a bigger plan for this young Nigerian.

Around the camp, the refugees called her "Biblia" when they did not know her name for she was the one who brought Bibles and hope to this hopeless place.

One day, she knocked on the door of one of the rooms. "Hello, my name is Rosemary, and I have Bibles if you would like one," she said.

The people in the room almost gasped in disbelief. "We just prayed that God would send us someone to teach us!" Even Muslims, living in the camp, were willing to listen to what this foreign woman had to say and many came to embrace Christ.

The refugee camp, being a melting pot of cultures, provided an opportunity for Rosemary and others from the Debrecen church to minister to people from Sudan, Iraq, Afghanistan, Ethiopia, Iran, Somalia, Jordan, Syria, Pakistan, Liberia, and many other lands. The Lord commands us to go to all the world and make disciples, and it was as if all the world had been brought to Rosemary as she entered the gates to minister.

ORPHANS AND GYPSIES

Other ministries grew out of the church as well. Bodi headed up a ministry to an orphanage in a city about a two-hour drive away. Each Saturday he would bring a team of believers to play games and teach the Bible to the children there. In time, God led members of the congregation to begin an outreach to a Roma (Gypsy) community. The church as a whole found itself deeply invested in meeting

The Gypsy community

the community's needs both physically and spiritually.

Outreach and ministry became synonymous with discipleship as God chose to use even the newest believers as instruments of His love, light, and hope to those facing the most hopeless of situations.

JUST PRAY ABOUT IT

In the fall of 1999, Christian took Bodi aside, "Bodi, I hate to say it, but it looks like we will be moving back to the States in the spring," Christian placed his hand on the medical student's shoulder. "And I really think God has chosen you to take over as pastor of this church."

"No, not me!" Bodi blurted out, stepping back and shaking his head defensively. "I am in my last year of medical school. I am going to be a doctor!" He felt trapped, and no one was going to force him into something like this. No way!

"Hey, it's okay." Christian realized the straightforward way he had mentioned this was overwhelming his friend.

"I want to serve God," Bodi clarified. "But I should do something in the medical field, like medical missions."

"Hey, relax," Christian reassured his friend. "I'm just saying, I believe God is going to call you to be a pastor somewhere, some day. You should pray about it."

Although the conversation shook up the soon-to-be doctor, it also got his attention. *Maybe I should be praying about what God wants me to do,* he thought to himself.

PLANS OF THE HEART

For I know the thoughts that I think toward you, says the
LORD, thoughts of peace and not of evil, to give you a future
and a hope. (Jeremiah 29:11–NKJV)

The truth was that Bodi already had a plan, a dream.
He figured he could make a lot more money in the medical field in the United States. And being fluent in English,
why shouldn't he? After all, he could go work in America
for five years and make enough money to come back and
do whatever he wanted without worrying about compen-
sation. Then he could do medical missions anywhere in
the world. Now poised to become a doctor within months,
that dream seemed so close to reality he could taste it.

But the accomplished medical student knew he should
pray. What if God had another plan? He would not want
to thwart that.

Bodi continued plowing through his final year of medical school while leading the weekly orphanage ministry
and attending every Bible study he could find. He found
himself at that critical turning point between university
and career, on which the course of his life would hinge.

And then one day he got a job offer. Not just "a" job
offer. This was "the" job of a lifetime for a young doctor.
He had been invited to Amsterdam for a position earning
more money than he could have made as a doctor in the
States. His heart leapt as he read the letter. It was a dream
come true. He could do this for a while and then come
back and do whatever he wanted! He was set.

He prayed and thanked God, amazed that the Lord would open such a door as this for him. But as the days passed, he grew perplexed. This was his dream, beyond anything he dared to dream, so why did this dull, nagging feeling grip his spirit every time he started to move forward with it? It was so right, and yet on a deeper level there grew the unshakable sense that something about it was so wrong.

Bodi committed it to prayer. "God, you know this is the sort of thing I've always wanted," he prayed in the quietness of his room. "But if you have another plan for me, I'll give it up. I'm yours."

DOES NOT MAKE SENSE

"Maybe God is calling me to be a pastor," Bodi commented to Christian one day. The young pastor grinned, glad to see his friend finally discovering what everyone else had known for years.

"But it just doesn't make sense," Bodi thought aloud. "Why would God take me through all these years of medical school if He was calling me to be a pastor?"

Christian sat down across from the soon-to-be doctor. "Bodi, I don't have all the answers, but God does everything for a reason."

Bodi leaned back in his chair thinking deeply. He had been reading the biography of Martyn Lloyd-Jones, an English doctor turned pastor. A quote from one of the man's sermon stirred Bodi's heart and plagued his mind:

"We [doctors] but spend most of our time rendering people fit to go back to their sin! I saw men on their sick beds, I spoke to them of their immortal souls, they promised grand things. Then they got better and back they went to their old sin! I saw I was helping these men to sin and I decided that I would do no more of it. I want to heal souls. If a man has a diseased body and his soul is all right, he is all right to the end; but a man with a healthy body and a diseased soul is all right for 60 years or so and then he has to face an eternity of hell. Ah, yes! we have sometimes to give up those which are good for that which is the best of all—the joy of salvation and newness of life." (D. Martyn Lloyd-Jones: The First Forty Years, 1899-1939, *by Iain Murray*)

It was becoming clear in Bodi's mind what he must do.

Christian looked at his friend with great affection. He wondered if now was the time to bring it up again. "Look, I don't want to put pressure on you or anything, but you know I'm leaving in April. Would you pray about whether you are the guy to take over?"

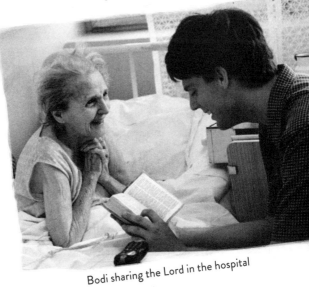

Bodi sharing the Lord in the hospital

Bodi nodded. His whole life seemed to hang in the balance. His choice right here and now would set his life on its course. And he wanted it to be the right one. He took a deep breath.

"You know when you first talked to me about this in the fall, you kind of scared me."

Christian laughed. "Yeah, I could tell."

"Now I have every reason to say no. I mean, I've got this job offer, my medical degree is practically complete." He scratched his head. "And yet I really think God does want me here as pastor. I want to heal more than people's physical bodies. I want to heal souls."

For the next months, between exams in internal medicine and neurology, Christian trained Bodi on how to lead the church. The transition between pastors flowed seamlessly as Bodi expanded the scope of his ministry and God expanded His grace.

UNEXPECTED INVITATION

One day Bodi got a call from the Hungarian Reformed Church in Ukraine. "I understand you are not just a pastor, you are a medical doctor as well," the man commented. "That is why we would like to invite you to come talk to our youth about depression."

Bodi happily accepted the invitation. But his expertise and advice on dealing with depression would not be gleaned from medical journals or his years in medical school. His source text would be the Word of God. Bodi grinned as he hung up the phone. Now he knew why God had called him to complete medical school. Simply being a pastor would not qualify him to speak under the auspices of the historic Hungarian Reformed Church. He needed credentials. And his medical degree provided those credentials. Those two letters, "Dr.," which stood before his name, would be God's key to unlock doors of opportunity to share the gospel in countless situations.

This invitation led to many future trips over the border into Ukraine. Before Bodi returned, he had spoken to more than 1,300 youth about not only depression, but also God's plan for sexuality and, of course, everything centered on the gospel of grace.

EXPANDING GRACE

Over the years that followed, Golgota Debrecen's relationship with Hungarian churches in Ukraine grew. Bodi's medical credentials led to many medical outreaches as doctors in training from the university, who attended the church, joined him to reach out and help those so desperately in need.

Besides the youth of the Reformed church, their Ukraine outreaches included supporting a Roma congregation, and later a leper colony. The Debrecen church planted other congregations in surrounding cities, including Nyíregyháza and Eger. It was clear that God was broadening the church borders and enlarging His territory into new communities. The grace that God began pouring out on this part of the world as the Iron Curtain fell was now expanding.

11

RETURNING GRACE

Now to Him who is able to do far more abundantly than all that we ask or think, according to the power at work within us, to Him be glory in the church and in Christ Jesus throughout all generations, forever and ever. Amen.

EPHESIANS 3:20-21

"Hello, Greg?" I made the long-distance phone call from California to Budapest. "This is Phil Metzger. I believe God is calling me back to Hungary."

I had left Esztergom after a good year of service in 1993-1994, right about the time the church in Budapest began. I came home to California with dreams of a pastoral job that never materialized. So instead of serving in a church, I found myself working and going to college, but the call towards missions still pulled at my heart.

No longer that eager teenager who traipsed the globe, I now had a wife and a child. I had gained ministry experience serving as a youth pastor under the guidance of Pastor Chuck Smith at Calvary Chapel Costa Mesa, leading worship and sometimes teaching a group of around 400 teens.

God had brought me through some basic training. Even though we had received two other pastoral offers, my wife, Joy, and I knew the Lord was calling us to overseas missions.

"That's radical!" Greg responded in his signature California style that he had become known for all over the country. "Dude, you know, there's this awesome couple, George and Icu. They're from Subotica, but are now living in a city called Kaposvár down in the south of Hungary," Greg explained. "They've served at the Castle in Austria and both have such a great heart for the Lord. They want to see a church planted in Kaposvár," Greg paused a moment. "Think this is what God is calling you to do?"

NEW FRIENDS

I quickly, yet prayerfully, contacted the couple and by the spring my family and I were on a twelve-hour flight to Hungary.

After all the air travel, we pushed through the jet lag, loaded our suitcases and 1-year-old daughter, Karina, aboard a bus for the three-hour ride down to Kaposvár. As the bus left Budapest and the Hungarian countryside passed by us, Joy began to doze on my shoulder. But I was not going to miss a moment. The adrenalin surged through my veins. My mind raced with all the possibilities the Lord might have for us.

At the bus station in Kaposvár, George and Icu Kolesnikov greeted us with their little boy in tow. "Sziasztok!" George welcomed, with his jovial greeting. His aura of hospitality immediately put us at ease. Having fled Subotica, Yugoslavia during the war, George and Icu stood as a flesh-and-blood testimony of God's work and deliverance. At their time serving at the Castle in Austria, Icu had fed the masses with her culinary skills, and George did just about everything else. This strong Hungarian was a little like a superhero. He could fix the plumbing and at the same time translate a Bible study into three different languages.

Remarkable people, Joy and I both thought in our hearts when we said goodbye to our new friends that first night.

SOWING SEEDS

Like farmers who plant their fields in expectation of a harvest, George and I began sowing seeds of faith on the streets of Kaposvár. We would talk to anyone who would listen, and God blessed our efforts, bringing a small number of souls to Himself.

Small, but sweet, the little group of new believers caused me to feel as if we were living in a New Testament church in the book of Acts. We met in a small,

Me and my family with Icu and George

unassuming apartment to study the Word, and the group just loved being together. It truly felt like family.

Eventually the little congregation outgrew the tiny apartment, and we started renting a room in the city.

BRAVING THE STORM

The rain poured down in torrents as the time of the midweek Bible study approached. "Do you think anyone will come tonight?" I asked George as we unlocked the room and turned on the lights.

"It's hard to say," George responded as he optimistically began to set up some chairs.

The culture was not one of automobiles and covered parking garages. Everyone went by foot, so the weather proved to be a significant factor affecting attendance.

As we finished setting up, we gazed out the window at the storm. It wasn't letting up. I sighed, beginning to face the reality that tonight was one big bust.

Suddenly, a woman entered the door with her son, a young blind man.

"Sziasztok!" I greeted these new folks with the best accent I could muster. I quickly introduced myself and George did the same, expressing how much we appreciated them coming out on such a wet night.

"Oh, I'm not staying," the woman said, as water dripped from her umbrella. "I just came to drop off my son, János. When will you be done?"

The woman went on her way as George and I spent the evening getting to know János.

Born with medical complications that cost him his sight, the young man never counted his blindness as a deficiency or handicap. He read in braille with a speed and agility that rivaled any seeing person, and he had a keen mind and remarkable talents. He had even taught himself how to play the guitar.

"So how did you come to know the Lord?" George asked.

"Well, I found Jesus when I was attending this one church," the young man explained. "But they kept telling me that God wanted to heal my sight." The young man shrugged his shoulders. "They prayed over me again and again, but I was never able to see anything."

George and I looked at each other and then back at János sympathetically.

"After awhile, I began to feel, well, kind of like I wasn't so welcome in the church," he continued.

"I get it," I said, patting János on his back. "They thought that believers have to be healed of all sickness. And you kind of contradicted their theology."

We wanted to surround János with love and fellowship. We truly enjoyed him, and he must have enjoyed us too because before long, János stood at the front of services leading the praise and worship. His testimony and talents challenged the congregation to reach for new heights with the Lord and tied an already close-knit congregation even closer.

Zsolt with his crazy hair months after becoming a Christian

SEEING WITH THE SOUL

Six months into the church plant we planned another outreach. On the day of the event, the music poured through the streets. My heart was overjoyed as I watched these new believers speak with people as they paused to watch the music and dramas.

My smile fell into a frown of concern as a small gang of leather-clad guys approached the event. My eyes widened as I evaluated the threat. Spikes shot out of the leather, and the chains they wore as jewelry could (and likely did) double as weapons. The fire of anger that flashed in the eyes of one with red spiky hair sent a chill down my spine.

Honestly, I was thinking, *These guys are going to kill me!* I managed to avoid interaction.

Thirty minutes later, the scariest one marched through the crowd as if he were looking for someone. He came right up to me. "Are you the pastor?" he asked.

I gulped and nodded as my life began to flash before my eyes.

"I just asked Jesus to come into my life, and that blind guy, János, told me I should come talk to you," as he pointed ed across the crowd.

I dropped my head and laughed and then looked back up at my new scary friend. I placed my hand on his shoulder and welcomed him to the family of God. How ironic that it took a blind man to help a young pastor see that a scary thug was really just a soul in need of a Savior.

DISCIPLESHIP

The spiky-haired guy's name was Zsolt, and it was no wonder his eyes had flashed with such rage. Life had given him much to be angry about. He had grown up in an orphanage with little love, kindness, or moral compass. It had been a rough life, but now he knew that God had not forgotten him. In Zsolt's early months as a believer, I spent time with him every day. We would read through the Proverbs together, and as I gave him instruction in the faith, Zsolt helped me develop my Hungarian language skills.

At that time in Hungary, all young men were required by law to serve in the military, and soon Zsolt's time came. But his days in the Army were short-lived as a problem with his hand got him sent home for surgery.

"I'm going crazy in this hospital. I'm so bored!" the young man complained on the phone to me one afternoon.

"Why don't you just start reading the Bible all the way through?"

A week later Zsolt called me again. "Okay, I read the whole Bible, now what?" he asked.

My jaw dropped. The young man had already read the entire Bible. He just could not get enough of the Word of God.

MEANINGFUL MINISTRY

The small congregation had an unquenchable hunger for God and a longing to serve others with His love. We took every opportunity we could to share the gospel: on the streets, at orphanages, an elderly home, and at the nearby U.S. military base. God even opened doors to allow us to serve in a daycare for handicapped children.

To help with the work, a couple of dynamic, fun-loving young men, one of whom I had mentored in my youth group years before, joined us in Kaposvár. Jason VanderBurgh had served as a youth pastor with me, and Jeremy Ampe had just graduated high school. Their presence brought a boost of energy, hilarious antics, and significant spiritual encouragement to all of us seeking to serve in Kaposvár as they plunged headfirst into outreach, language learning, and all kinds of ministry.

Although the ministries varied, the goal remained the same: to share the love of God and His plan of salvation for the world. At the daycare for handicapped children, it seemed natural that God would use the congregation to bring hope and encouragement to the parents, but God had something else in mind.

HOUSE OF SUNSHINE

"Sziasztok!" Ági Andriska welcomed us with a wide smile every time we entered "Napsugár," the "House of Sunshine," a wonderful daycare for disabled children. From the very beginning, it was clear to all of us that Ági was special. Ági had a way with children. She treated them with honor and taught them how to deal with their various disabilities. She saw the children through eyes of compassion, not condescension. It was easy to love Ági, because she so loved those kids.

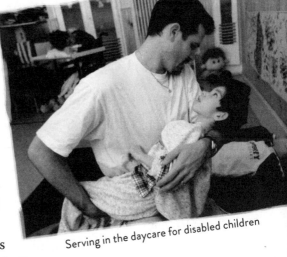

Serving in the daycare for disabled children

After several months of serving in this facility, we began an English learning program at the church. Kaposvár was full of people who wanted to learn English, so it seemed like a natural ministry. We invited Ági to come and were not surprised at all when she showed up. Over the next couple of months Ági began learning basic English, and we were able to share Jesus with her.

On Thanksgiving Day, we decided to teach our students a little American culture by having a party to celebrate the holiday. And indeed there was much to be thankful for. Amidst the talk of turkey and stuffing, pumpkin pie, and cranberry sauce, Ági surrendered her life to Jesus. The precious teacher at the "House of Sunshine" now had the Son of God shining through her.

EXPANDING FAMILY

My family expanded as the years passed with the birth of our baby boy, Judah.

When Judah was 6-months-old and Karina was 4, a member of our little church brought a delightful little girl with her to the service. Her name was Niki. When Joy and I learned the charming 8-year-old lived in an orphanage and had been there since her mother died when she was 5, we felt compelled to spend more time with her. Niki and Karina became the best of friends, and as a result, Niki became a regular weekend visitor at the Metzger home.

Little Karina grew to love Niki like a sister. And the precocious 4-year-old could clearly see a solution to all her friend's troubles. One night, as Joy and I tucked her into bed, Karina prayed, "Lord, thank you that Niki needs parents, and my mom and dad are parents." The little girl's blond locks framed her angelic face as her prayer became more intense. "Thank you that we could adopt Niki."

We appreciated Karina's tender heart, but adoption had never been in the equation. It's not that we were averse to it; we simply had never seriously considered it. We laughed about how sweet it was that our little girl would want us to adopt Niki, but we put no more thought into it.

As the months passed, Niki began to feel more and more like part of our family. It just felt like she belonged. Finally, one day Joy and I woke up to the reality that in our hearts, we already saw Niki as one of ours. "Why haven't we adopted her already?" we asked each other. The process took about nine months, and in 2002 Niki officially became a Metzger. We were finally given the privilege to call her our own.

Sometimes, when people hear our story, they comment about how lucky a Hungarian orphan was to find an

American family. But we know better. In reality, we know we are the lucky ones. We know that Niki, just like each one of our biological children, is a true gift from heaven.

MOVING ON

In 2001, I began to sense that our time in Kaposvár was coming to a close. The vision the Lord had given us was to plant a church and raise up nationals to take over the work. The truth was that George was more than capable of running this church with excellence. I really wasn't needed there anymore and that was a good thing. We began to pray about where the Lord would have us go next as we formally handed the church over to George and Icu in September of that year.

We knew God wasn't finished with us in Hungary. We would simply embark on a new adventure as God's hand of grace continued to move in our lives and in this land.

WHAT'S NEXT?

The thought of what was next had not really entered our mind when we first felt George was meant to take over the church. Once we had announced to our small congregation that we would be leaving everyone was asking us, "Where are you going?" We were not sure what to say. We were worn out from planting a new church. It was an amazing privilege, but it was physically and emotionally taxing.

Joy and I weren't sure whether we were supposed to move to another city in Hungary and start over again, or do something else. We were open to anything. In fact, when

CHURCH PLANTING

I like to refer to church planting like launching a rocket. When the countdown finishes, the rockets fire and smoke fills the whole area. It is a huge explosion of energy, and at first the rocket does not seem to go anywhere.

The amount of energy that it takes to put a rocket into space is amazing. That is how church planting feels. Sometimes there is a lot of energy going out but not a lot of movement. You can start to wonder if anything you are doing is making a difference.

Over time you stand back in awe as you see how the Lord impacts lives, hearts, and communities as the gospel is being preached and the Word of God is being taught. Lives are changed, and you are reminded afresh that His Word says, "How then will they call on Him in whom they have not believed? And how are they to believe in Him of whom they have never heard? And how are they to hear without someone preaching?" (Romans 10:14)

a friend back in America offered to help move us back to the U.S. and get us set up there, we seriously considered it.

For the next several weeks we toyed around with the idea of leaving Hungary and going back to the States, but there was an uneasiness inside. It all sounded great, but something was not right. I was talking to a pastor in America, and his encouragement helped us make our decision. He said, "You know there are a lot of people willing to pastor a church in the States but not so many where you are." His words really struck me, and so we committed to more prayer over the next step of our journey.

One night I sensed the Lord speaking to me. "What do you want to do?" I guess up to this point I had not really asked the question. *What do I want to do?* I was too busy trying to do what I thought God wanted me to do without having any clarity or direction. So when I sensed God asking me what I wanted to do, I had to really think about it. We dreamed of seeing Hungarians raised up to start churches across this region. Instead of Joy and me going out and starting a new church, we wanted to invest in discipling Hungarians who were called by God to plant churches.

The next day my good buddy, Rod Thompson, called. "Hey, I heard you turned the church over to George. What are you gonna do next?"

"I have no idea, but I think we need to stay in Europe," I said.

Rod responded, "Why don't you pray about joining us at the new Bible college that we are opening in Hungary this year? And you could pray about starting a Hungarian program for the school to help equip them for ministry and church planting."

I honestly could not believe Rod's words. It was exactly what we believed God was calling us to do. We had not even thought about the Bible college as an option, but once he said it, it seemed the perfect place.

"I'll pray!" I told him, but in my heart I already knew the answer. I called him back that same day, and we committed to the next step of the journey.

BUILDING A BIBLE COLLEGE

Do your best to present yourself to God as one approved, a worker who has no need to be ashamed, rightly handling the Word of truth.

2 TIMOTHY 2:15

Australia... blue skies, sandy beaches. Tamás Gémes flipped through the magazine featuring the place of his dreams. He had graduated university with a degree in architecture and now worked in his field at a company called Graphisoft in Budapest. Graphisoft had a branch in Australia. And they were open to him making the transition within the company. It was as if the Lord was orchestrating it with His own hand, to give him the desires of his heart. He could really end up in Australia someday, maybe even someday soon!

Tamás had to work out the details through the embassy.

"Pray for me. I am going to the embassy again this week to work on the Australia thing!" Tamás told his pastor, Greg, in Budapest. He had been trying to work through the bureaucracy for eight months now and each time he had been met with a resounding no. Greg and Mike Montgomery did pray for their friend, Tamás, but what Tamás did not know then is that they earnestly prayed that God would not allow him to go.

As a young adult just starting out in his life and career, Tamás genuinely sought God's leading for the path he should travel. He believed, or at least had hoped, that being an Australian architect fulfilled some part of that plan, so he pursued each and every possibility. Then one day, everything fell apart.

"Ring! Rrrrring!" It was Monday morning and Tamás fumbled for his phone. "Hello?"

"Hello, Tamás?" It was someone from his company.

"Yes?" the young architect responded, surprised to get a call so early.

"I'm afraid we have some bad news. Graphisoft has done some downsizing, and it looks like your whole department is being eliminated."

"What?" Tamás almost dropped the phone. It was out of the blue. He was preparing to move up and out to Australia within this company. And now he had been let go.

CHAPTER 12

LETTING GO

"Whoever finds his life will lose it, and whoever loses his life for My sake will find it." (Matthew 10:39)

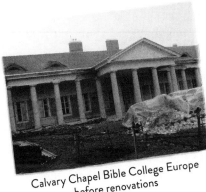

Calvary Chapel Bible College Europe before renovations

Like sand slipping through his fingertips, in an instant he had lost it all: his job, his plans, his dream. Tamás took a deep breath. He felt broken inside.

"Okay, Lord," he sighed. "Obviously You have a different plan for my life. I have no choice but to let go of my plan now."

The following Sunday Tamás went to church as he did each week, hoping Greg's study would provide some inspiration as to where he should go and what he should do. He slouched down in his seat and prepared to open his Bible, when Greg made an unexpected announcement.

"I am so stoked about what God is doing in Hungary!" Greg announced.

Tamás smiled at his pastor's California slang. It never got old.

"Just this week Calvary Chapel bought an old manor house in Hungary that will become our Bible college for Central Europe."

Tamás pushed his long, blonde bangs out of his eyes as he sat up to listen more closely as Greg continued.

"If anyone has time to come out and help us with renovations, let me know."

The unemployed architect's eyes widened. *Renovations? I'm an architect! I could help with this,* he thought to himself.

And so Tamás moved down to Vajta, about 90 miles south of Budapest. He thought he would stay and help out for about three months but ended up staying three years.

CHALLENGE AND CHANGE

The "Castle" in Millstatt, Austria, served as a training ground for Eastern Europeans, and it had served well during the late 1980s and early 1990s. Countless students flooded into the picturesque Austrian town and scarcely was a room vacant. In fact, the place was proving to be too small for the job. So it was time to start looking for something else.

Push came to shove when changes in visa laws began to block students from being able to go there. In the wake of the fallen Iron Curtain, many Austrians resented the flow of easterners into the West. As a result, the new harsh visa laws brought an abrupt end to the Castle's original purpose of training Christian leaders from the East.

The "something else" came in the form of an old manor house known as the Zichy Kastély, in a little Hungarian village called Vajta. Calvary Chapel Bible College Europe prepared to move to Hungary, and the Castle in Austria continued to serve as a conference center.

It was also a season of challenge and change for the novice architect who found himself thrown into the enormous task of renovating the old mansion. The crumbling structure stood as a pale shadow of its former glory. It had been built in 1922 by the aristocratic Zichy family, one of the five richest families in Hungary in the early 1900s. The wealthy family lived in the mansion only two months out of every year. During these months they would stay to oversee their property holdings in the surrounding area.

But those years of decadence would be short lived. After World War II, the Zichy family fled to Sweden as the communists moved in and confiscated all such grand estates "for the good of the people." The estate was then used as a vacation spot for communist leaders and their families for seven years, and afterwards it served as a camp for disabled children. When the Iron Curtain fell in 1989, the bureaucratic chaos meant that there was no money for maintenance. The already aged structure began falling apart and eventually was abandoned.

Tamás had his work cut out for him, and so did I. Having just wrapped up my time in Kaposvár and handed the church over to George and Icu, I moved my family to Vajta. God had brought together an eclectic group of builders to renovate this place, and they all put their heart and soul into the project.

Under the dusty floor, we could make out the small art deco, black-and-white tiles which testified to the structure's former majesty, a time long since forgotten. Large cracks ran through the plastered walls. There was so much work to be done. Could we really have it ready in the next few months before the first students arrive?

I walked up to one of the beautiful, yet weathered wooden cabinets with black lacquered trimmings and pulled open the door. Out fell the carcass of a huge bird. The whole place was just dilapidated and dingy. Most of us Californians wore flip-flops (affectionately called Jesus sandals here) when weather permitted. But that changed in those early months of construction as we discovered that the tall grass and the basement had become infested with snakes.

Between drawings and architectural plans, assisting in the renovations and directing workers, Tamás found himself in a unique time in his life. Stuck in a village with a total of 300 houses and a total population of only 800 people, there was not a lot for a young adult to do for fun. So he started taking a deeper look at the Word of God. For the first time in his life he had the time to really study the Scriptures systematically, chapter-by-chapter.

And so God began to disciple a young architect beneath the plaster and the paint. As Tamás cast a new vision for an old mansion, God cast a new calling for Tamás' life.

SCHOOL BEGAN

The Bible college after renovation

In the summer of 2002, the entire Bible college made its move from Austria to Hungary. An old friend and Hungary veteran, Rod Thompson, orchestrated the seemingly insurmountable task. He brought along another familiar face, Paul Lange, who had joined the teaching staff at the college in Austria several years earlier. Along with Robin Turner and Mark Walsh, teachers at the Castle in Austria, the leadership team for the new ministry in Hungary was complete. It was as if things had come full circle. Having plowed the ground and sown the

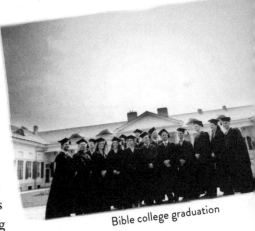

Bible college graduation

seeds, these guys returned to the country they loved in order to train young believers to lead the next generation to Christ.

A NEW CALLING

The students arrived in the fall of 2002 ready to study the Word, discover missions, and find God's call for their lives. But they found themselves entering dorm rooms with beds still in boxes—some assembly required.

So before pouring over their Bibles, they would have to build their beds. The good-spirited students, eager to lend a hand, willingly grabbed the screwdrivers. And so in their first semester in Hungary, they also helped build the Bible college.

As the students assisted with the final touches of the building, the architect joined the ranks of the academics. Tamás stayed on as a student at the college. When I taught Bible studies, he often translated for me and I could see something happening.

"I think God's going to make you into a pastor," I told him one day after the study.

"Yeah, right!" he laughed.

Tamás soon forgot our conversation, but I remember it vividly because I could see that God was doing a real work in him. And I was not alone. God was taking an architect of buildings and transforming him into a fisher of men. After his year in Bible college, he stayed on as an intern, as God trained him for a future he had never even considered.

A NEW SCHOOL YEAR

Meanwhile, Calvary Chapel Bible College Europe became a place of growth and transformation for countless students discovering God's call. In 2003, Zoli came in with the band of new students eager to see what God might have in store for them.

Zoli came to Christ when he was about 20 years old through some American friends living in his hometown of Dunaújváros. He had become involved in Golgota Budapest over the years and now was ready to go deeper. But that road would not be an easy one.

TRAGEDY

The LORD is near to the brokenhearted and saves the crushed in spirit. (Psalm 34:18)

"I've got to go home," Zoli's face had fallen sickly pale after he hung up the phone. He rushed from the room, and everyone knew that something was horribly wrong.

"Zoli, what's wrong? Where you going?" a fellow student asked, but Zoli dashed by not even hearing the words.

Fumbling to grab a few things from his room, Zoli wasted no time. In minutes he was gone. We would later learn that his father had committed suicide, and his mother had found his body.

Such a tragedy cannot help but leave cold, dark doubts and questions in the heart of anyone. It's a process, a journey that must be walked through in grace and honesty. But Zoli felt he had to be stronger than all that. He was a Christian. He had read the whole Bible more than once. He was preparing to serve God in some great way. And so,

SUICIDE

Psychologist Margot Honti said about Hungarians, "We know what it is to be losers. We have all been losers for centuries." [1] This was a part of her response when asked to explain the Hungarian soul.

In 2012, Hungary had the 6th highest rate of suicide in the world. Sadly, this number is considered a positive change because it was nearly double that in 1984. In that year, Hungary had the largest percentage of suicides and to this day it is still the highest ever recorded in the world. The suicide rate of Hungary is nearly 4x that of the United States.

---

[1] F. Branfman, "In Search of the Hungarian Soul," Budapest Week, 6–12 February 1992, p. 11

instead of talking it all out, he buried his doubts and anger deep within himself and pretended they did not exist. He would not be weak, he determined.

But under that amazing mask of trumped-up faith, deep in the hidden places of his soul, bitterness took root and slowly yet steadily began to choke out his relationship with God. Still, Zoli wore the mask well. He preached grace, witnessed often, read his Bible, and even prayed regularly. *Yes, God is pretty lucky to have someone like me who can handle tragedy and not wane in these areas,* he thought

Despite his hidden pain and not-so-hidden pride, God still poured out His grace on Zoli. He finished Bible college, became an assistant pastor, and even taught some classes at the school. When Chuck Smith came to speak at the Bible college, the leadership chose Zoli to serve as translator. He had moved up the "ranks" and had really become somebody. He felt he had earned it because he was the most devoted Christian he knew.

But roots of bitterness, like weeds, do not just go away. They fester just below the surface choking out new life by cutting it off from the source. It was just a matter of time.

HOLY SPIRIT

Zoli scratched his head through his thick dark hair as he poured over his Bible. His eyebrows furrowed as he shook his head and sighed, "I just don't get this Holy Spirit thing."

"What don't you get about it?" I asked. I could tell something about it was really bothering him.

"All this stuff about the 'baptism' or 'filling' or 'gift' of the Holy Spirit. I just don't get it. That's never happened to me." He explained. "I don't buy it. I think the Holy Spirit comes at the moment a person puts his faith in Jesus and that's it."

"Well, sure. It can happen that way. For some people it does," I explained. "But the Holy Spirit can fill someone as a later experience too."

"But I have a real problem with this," the young man said almost defiantly. "I can't teach this stuff if I have never experienced it."

"Hey, relax," I tried to calm him. "You know this is not a salvation issue."

But Zoli would not let it go. He became all the more fixated on the doctrine. He let it consume him so much that he began isolating himself. But the problem was not just the Holy Spirit. There was anger and bitterness he had been bottling up for years.

DOWNWARD SPIRAL

One's pride will bring him low, but he who is lowly in spirit will obtain honor. (Proverbs 29:23)

Still bound up in his own pride, and therefore unwilling to seek help, Zoli began to spin out of control. He could feel himself slipping further and further away from God. He no longer knew how to discern the voice of God. Each idea and thought that raced through his head became a struggle. *Was that from God? Was that from me? Was that just temptation?*

Frustration and anger welled up inside him. These emotions seemed to explode from nowhere. He had to find some sort of outlet just to keep himself sane. He needed a break from it all—a way to forget. He could think of only one thing that might give him what he needed. And in the silent hours of night, he began secretly perusing the Internet for pornography and entered into a world where he could forget everything for a moment.

But the moments were never enough. First he only allowed himself to indulge when he was at home for the weekend. But he needed more. The anger and the frustration still existed. In fact, they grew more intense. So he began sneaking onto the computers of the college when no one was around and seeking relief in sin.

PORNOGRAPHY

There is no point in highlighting the plague of pornography in Hungary alone. This is a universal plague that has infected every part of life from the boardroom to the classroom. Pornography is a multibillion-dollar industry that has added to an increase in child abuse, prostitution, and human trafficking globally.

For many, pornography begins as a curiosity or a diversion, but it quickly becomes an addiction. Christian men, and women, are struggling to be set free and to get right with God. They are dealing with so much shame, guilt and regret, which oftentimes takes them right back to the very sins they are trying to be set free from.

EXPOSED

"Zoli, we need to have a talk." I motioned for him to follow me. We walked into the sanctuary at the college and began with some small talk. "Zoli, our IT director noticed some websites on your account and brought it to my attention." We talked about the danger of pornography. We talked about the grace of God and forgiveness.

"As your friend, Zoli, I want you to know that we all love you and want to see you healthy." I said. "As your pastor, I want you to know that there is so much grace and love from God for you, but as your boss, I need you to know that this can't happen here. You can't be looking at porn and be serving in the role that you are in."

Zoli agreed to the terms and stayed on at the Bible college for another semester. But that was just prolonging the inevitable. By the time summer of 2006 rolled around, he had become so unhappy that he felt he had to go home. The village of Vajta made him miserable. He no longer liked the Bible college. He was ready to break free from Golgota and the way we do things. He decided he would return to his hometown and serve God there on his own terms, and then everything would be better. Then he would have peace, he thought.

Zoli left without giving proper notice, reciting religious axioms like, "God told me to do this so I can't delay in obeying Him." But that was really just a cop out. Confused and arrogant, he set out to do things his own way.

COLD, HARD REALITY

Unfortunately, a change in geography would not cure Zoli's ailments. He moved home only to discover that all the misery and angst followed him. He found no more peace at home than at the Bible college.

His heart began beating loudly in his chest and hands trembled. Panic rushed through his veins. *What's wrong with me,* he wondered. *If leaving that place didn't solve my problems, then what's really wrong?* He agonized deep within his soul. Maybe it was all a lie from the very beginning. *Maybe I was never saved. Maybe there's no such thing as salvation!*

Zoli buried his face in his pillow as he lay on his bed. Despair gripped him as one thought dominated his mind: *I'm lost! I'm done!* And a voice echoed through the recesses of his mind saying, "You lied to yourself for five years, but now the mask has fallen!"

A cold breeze blew over his body, sending a chill down his spine. He felt his heart grow cold, as all the love that once filled him seemed to melt away into nothingness. Within hours every warm, kind, or positive thought he carried had drained away. All love inside him had disintegrated, even his love for his mother and grandmother. In the days that followed, he walked the rooms of his mother's home like a wisp. He held the appearance of a man; he could eat and breathe, but inside there was nothing but emptiness. All life was gone.

HELL ON EARTH

The way he saw it, he only had two choices. He could end it all and take his own life, just like his own father had done years earlier. Or he could pretend that these last five years of following Jesus had never happened. He opted for the latter, beginning a "hell on earth" journey that would last more than five years.

He had chosen to completely separate himself from God and all that God is. All that remained for him was hell, and he plunged himself into it. Alcohol, drugs, the party scene—those things never held a fascination for him. But sex, well, that was a different story.

With nothing to hold him back, he started to regularly watch pornography on television and the Internet. It provided a good way to attempt to forget. But soon naked bodies on the screen were not enough. He felt driven to take it further. Maybe if he could just have "the real thing," then he would be satisfied. Getting a girlfriend really was not an option. He didn't want a relationship. He hated being around people. He hated everyone, perhaps himself most of all. Prostitutes represented the only real solution.

Like a thirsty man guzzling salt water, Zoli gorged himself with that which could not satisfy, but rather only destroy him. *I'm going to suffer for eternity so I might as well have fun now,* he told himself as he called his next prostitute.

Such "fun" always disappeared all too quickly, and then Zoli would awaken to find himself facing another miserable day, disgusted with the man he saw in the mirror.

Deep down inside, he knew that God waited for him. He had learned all the Scriptures at the Bible college. Jesus offered salvation to sinners by grace. It was a gift, but he did not want a gift. No, he outright rejected it. If he was not good enough, if he could not earn it, then he would not take part in it at all!

Still sometimes, when the house stood quiet and still, thoughts of Christ's return would torment him. *What if it happened today?* he shuddered at the thought. He imagined standing before the judgment seat of Christ required to give an account of his life. The thought was terrifying.

Then he would shake his head and try to force the image out of his mind as he turned on the computer and searched for a new porn site in an attempt to obliterate the thoughts.

CHRISTMAS TRIP

And the Word became flesh and dwelt among us, and we have seen His glory, glory as of the only Son from the Father, full of grace and truth. (John 1:14)

Zoli had become a pathetic ghost of the man he used to be. Everyone could see it, but no one really knew how to help him. His sister who lived in Germany managed to convince him to come visit her for Christmas in 2011. She thought that some time away from Hungary, with her kids climbing all over him, would do Zoli some good.

The trip had been largely uneventful. Christmas came and went. They would leave to head back to the dreary monotony of daily life on December 28.

PROSTITUTION

Prostitution became legal in Hungary in 1999. Today, the government recognizes it as a legitimate form of business, issuing work permits for such enterprises and taxing them. Today 22% of the prostitutes in Hungary are younger than 18 years old. Although illegal, some girls get their start in this industry at as young as 13.

"Hey, let's watch a movie tonight," his sister suggested on his last night in town. "I've got this great one called *Walk the Line*."

"That's about Johnny Cash, right?" he asked and his sister nodded. "Yeah, I've seen that one, but it's good. I wouldn't mind seeing it again."

After the kids were in bed, they all gathered around the television and watched the movie. Before long, everyone grew tired and had gone to bed. Zoli sat by himself watching the movie in the darkness. As the story wrapped up, he leaned against the couch considering Johnny Cash's life. He thought about Johnny's marriage to June Carter and what it is to really live for the glory of God.

Then quite unexpectedly, words came into his mind, almost like a voice from inside. "You too can live a life that glorifies God, if you want to," the voice said. "You just need to turn back to God." Zoli wondered what was happening. He knew it was a moment of great significance. "Don't be ashamed to go back to God because of the fear of going to hell."

The young man paused for a moment and took inventory of his life. It had all become so dark and hopeless. *Why not try it? What do I have to lose,* he reasoned.

So he took a deep breath and started to pray, "God, we both know what kind of a person I am. You've always known it, but now I know it too. We both know that I am not coming to You because I'm this holy guy. In fact, I know I'm not even worthy to come to You. If there is a way that I could come back, will You receive me back?"

Suddenly he started crying right there in the dark living room. After several minutes he realized that he could not stop. *What's going on?* he thought to himself. Then he understood. *I am actually crying over my sins, and these are tears of repentance.* All the theology he had studied at the Bible college came rushing back to him. *And this is the presence of God!*

The tears grew into almost convulsive sobs. "I am nothing." He just kept saying those words over and over again. He buried his face into his pillow to avoid waking anyone up. "You are everything!" He had to keep saying it. "I am nothing; You are everything!"

After about an hour the weeping came to an end. He found himself lying in the bed facing the ceiling, wrapped in the warm security of knowing that God was there too. God had come and had forgiven his sins. They were really together in relationship again.

Zoli could almost physically feel the weight of his sins lifted from his chest. He could feel God reaching inside him and gently transforming his heart of stone into a loving heart.

A NEW LIFE

When Zoli arrived back home in Hungary, he raced for the Bible he had not touched in more than five years. For some reason, he began reading 1 Corinthians. When he got to 1 Corinthians 1:28, he could not believe his eyes. The Hungarian wording goes something like this: "God chose the nothing—to bring to nothing what is viewed as something." He immediately thought of his prayer the previous night: "I am nothing; You are everything!"

As he struggled to get his mind around what had happened to him, wondering if it was really real, God confirmed it in His Word. And God said to him, "Zoli, I am choosing you."

RETURN TO BIBLE COLLEGE

God's hand continued to move in Zoli's life, and he grew in humility and grace. Even the issue of the Holy Spirit, which had been such a stumbling block to him in years prior, now became an anchor of his soul and ministry as God filled him to overflowing, allowing him to experience more of the Spirit than he ever thought possible.

That same Holy Spirit broke the bonds of sin in his life and today empowers him to boldly serve as conference coordinator at the Bible college and as worship leader in a nearby church. God never gave up on Zoli. He now sits at the front desk of the college, with a sparkle in his dark eyes testifying to all the students who come through that God is a God of deliverance and He has chosen to do a remarkable work of grace in this man's heart.

ONE OF MANY

Zoli's story is just one of many occurring all over Eastern Europe as so many struggle to understand the depths of God's love for them. Without question, the doctrines of grace and forgiveness are the most impacting doctrines for Hungarians.

"Could God forgive me after having an abortion?" some ask in tears.

"I'm a prostitute, can God really love me?" others wonder in desperation.

"I've been addicted to pornography for so long, can God possibly set me free?" still others question.

The answer with God is always yes. He is the God of all grace, and absolutely nothing is impossible with Him.

TRANSFORMING GRACE

God called Rod Thompson back to America in 2005, and I had taken over as director of the Bible college in Vajta. While that kept my hands full, a pastor's heart still burned inside me. I needed to be close to the people. So when the opportunity arose in 2006 to lead an evening service in Budapest, I jumped at the opportunity. It had become a regular part of my weekly schedule and I loved it. "Hey Phil, can we sit down and talk?" Greg asked me after I taught the Sunday evening service at Golgota Budapest.

I knew Greg had been struggling with a lot of difficulties in his life, but I had no idea what kind of bombshell he was about to drop.

Greg preaching at Calvary Budapest

"Phil, I've been sensing a real change coming on," Greg said as he closed the door to his office. "I think that God is preparing me to go back to the States."

I didn't know what to say. The thought of Greg Opean leaving Hungary was a bit incomprehensible. God had used Greg as a source of wisdom and encouragement for so many of us for so many years. His presence as the guy God used to start it all meant a lot. *What would happen if he were gone?*

And then Greg really lowered the boom. "I think you are the guy to take over Golgota Budapest," he said.

I must have looked shell-shocked, sitting there with my mouth hanging open but no words coming out. I felt again like that gangly teenager in Esztergom so many years before whom Greg had asked to teach the Word. All I could do was wonder if I were capable or remotely worthy to do such a thing. But this was ten times more serious. God had His hand on Golgota Budapest. His Spirit moved in this place on a grand scale. *Could God really entrust someone like me with such responsibility?*

And if that were not overwhelming enough, I pondered what it would be like to try and fill Greg's shoes. My mind swarmed with thoughts of how I would be known as the guy who single-handedly destroyed this great church—and probably the college, too!

AFFIRMATION AND ASSURANCE

Just as I was becoming paralyzed with the thought of the disaster I could wreak, God's gentle Spirit reminded me that the church wasn't mine to mess up. Who was I to claim the ability to destroy what was not mine? Ministry is not about taking control of what belongs to God. It is about submitting to the Lord's leading in all things He has called us to.

The Lord also sent people to encourage me in taking this step, including giving me some wonderfully specific prophecies. Nobody was more encouraging than Greg himself. He believed that God had called me, and he did everything he could to assure a successful transition.

Both God and Greg wasted no time in moving forward with the transition. Only a month after I stopped struggling with God and officially said yes, I was standing before the church as their new pastor.

THE DAY OF TRANSITION

As I prepared for that day of transition, when we would say our goodbyes to Greg and the elders would pray over me as the new pastor, I hoped that God would give me a message for the future of the church. But the message God gave me left me nervous. Certain that God wanted me to share from the transition between Elijah and Elisha, I began to address the congregation with the story of two of the prophets in the Old Testament.

Just as Elisha asked for a double portion of the blessing God had placed on Elijah, I too asked God for a double portion. *Was I being presumptuous?* Maybe so, but I believe Elisha knew that he was half the man Elijah was

TRANSITIONS

I don't know what pastoral transitions are supposed to look like. I imagine there are books out there that discuss the process at length. We did not read those books. But in spite of our ignorance, God really worked.

A number of factors led to the success of the transition:

Church Elders. The elders committed their help and support from the moment Greg mentioned that he was leaving and that he felt I was to be his replacement. God used them to encourage me so much even though we were all wondering what was going to happen after Greg left.

Congregation. Though they were sad to see Greg depart, this gracious congregation accepted it as God's will and welcomed me with open arms. I hear that sometimes people leave the church when a new pastor arrives. As far as I know this did not happen. That's how welcoming these people were.

Leadership. Greg was secure in God's authority over the church, in his choice as a replacement, and in the congregation.

Calling. It was important that I be secure in my calling. We should not undertake any great work for God without the assurance that He has called us.

and would need double the blessing to do the job! I related to Elisha. I would need a double blessing of God to be able to do what He had called me to do in leading this amazing congregation.

I shared with the church that I believed that Golgota Budapest was the greatest church in the world and that I was honored to be their new pastor. I also expressed that I did not believe God called me to take over a work that was at its peak. I believed (and still do) that we were still discovering all that God wanted to do in the capital of Hungary. I expressed faith that God was going to more than double this church in every way—in numbers, in opportunities, and in depth. Honestly, the Lord has done above and beyond what we even thought possible.

One of the elders of Golgota Budapest said to me that day, "I did not expect that to be your message. Now I want to be here just to see what's going to happen!" I felt the same way. I want to be here to see all the Lord is going to do.

TROUBLES

But it would not all be smooth sailing for me. The week after I took over, the lawsuit that had been filed a year before (by the guy who ran the convenience store in our building) went to court. The judge actually ruled against us. A wave of shock rattled through the church board of elders. *What had we done wrong? Was this just the devil attacking us?* The questions plagued everyone's mind.

The reality was that the church had removed the man before the contract expired (even if by just a couple days). The elders had to face this fact. It was time to gather to pray to ask the Lord for forgiveness in wronging this man, and then to go ask the man himself for forgiveness.

Not surprisingly, the man wasn't interested in apologies. Collecting on the lawsuit was all that concerned him.

But for us the confession in prayer brought great peace. While dealing with this issue, we had a midweek service where we invited people to come up front for prayer. I prayed with one man who came forward. The Lord had touched him, and he was so glad to be getting his life back on track. As he turned to go back to his seat he made a passing comment: "By the way, I'm a lawyer, and I doubt you need one, but if you do I would love to help the church in any way I can." God always managed to provide exactly what the church needed when we needed it.

After the church lost the first court case, we appealed, hoping for a more sensible judgment. In the appeals court we won, which meant it would be sent back down to the first court. When the case came up for trial again, it fell to the same judge as before, and the church lost again. Years passed, the appeals continued. The amount the man sued us for grew to half a million American dollars!

Endurance and perseverance would prove critical in this battle. After eight years, the case came to its conclusion when the judge threw the case out, granting the church the final, long-fought after victory.

Meanwhile, the church blossomed in ministry as God continued to pour out His grace on the congregation and the whole city.

SEX INDUSTRY

Pornography, prostitution, and human trafficking plague the streets of Budapest. In 2005, 25% of all pornographic films produced in Europe originated in Hungary. By 2008, the porn industry in Hungary was generating more than $975 million a year. What's worse, this industry includes the exploitation of children as well as a booming human trafficking movement.

According to a U.S. State Department report in 2010, Hungary is not in compliance with the minimum standards for the elimination of trafficking. Many girls are taken from the East and sent to the West to work as sex slaves. Sadly, this means they travel through Hungary to get there.

PIMPS AND PROSTITUTES

Seeing the hardened faces of prostitutes on street corners in the night, some members of our congregation recognized a desperate need to bring hope to the city's prostitutes and started a ministry called "Table 22." The ministry is named from Matthew 22 where Jesus tells the parable of the wedding feast. A king had a son who was getting married, and they invited the most important people throughout the kingdom. However, they were not interested in attending, so the king sent his servants out to the streets to invite commoners to the wedding. Even though they were unworthy, they were clothed and fed by the king.

Today, Table 22 is making a difference in the city. We have seen girls and even their pimps give their lives to the Lord. People from the streets have been clothed in the righteousness of Christ and feast upon His grace.

HELP FOR THE HOMELESS

As with any major city, the streets of Budapest have become a home to many hopeless people who through bad choices or tragic circumstances have nowhere to live. Seeing these desperate souls huddled around trash cans or begging for food, some in the congregation felt compelled to reach out to them. This ministry began in prayer, asking God how we could make a difference. It is an overwhelming problem and helping has the potential of draining all resources and energies. As people prayed, God opened a door. Since 2006, Golgota Budapest has run a homeless shelter that feeds about 200 people each day. It is a place where those who are struggling can get a warm meal, a shower, and a bit of dignity. It is a place where they can hear about Jesus.

A CHURCH ALL AROUND THE CITY

Golgota North. In a city of nearly two million, the spiritual needs of the people are great. As a result, Golgota Budapest saw a need to become a "church all around the city" early on. In 2003, Golgota Budapest established a second congregation in the northern part of Budapest; it is called Golgota Békásmegyer. The Holy Spirit was moving in the youth group of an established church. Both the church and the young people agreed it would be best if they left the denominational umbrella and became an independent

GOOD DEEDS AND THE GOSPEL

Many churches in the inner city become more of a beacon of social help rather than preaching the message of Jesus Christ. This has always been a tension within gospel-centered churches. How much social work should we do? Should we do any at all?

We believe God called us to bring the gospel to save men's souls and allow God to transform their lives, as well as social help where people are suffering or have need. We cannot see our brothers in need and do nothing. What good is a message of God's great love for mankind without His people expressing that love to others? But at the same time, we are all about the gospel. As Paul said in 1 Corinthians 9:16, "Woe to me if I do not preach the gospel!"

But that's not to suggest we somehow have to earn God's favor by doing these good deeds. God knows the best way to use each of our lives. I think too often churches can place pressure on people to get involved and do something for God. Before we can really serve God, we need to allow God to change us. We cannot give to others what is not flowing out of our hearts. People who have allowed God to radically transform them create the most powerful ministries.

Golgota Budapest is far from a perfect church; it is a church filled with sinners, from the pulpit to the pews. The moral of this story of grace is not that a church or a movement reached a country. No person deserves the glory for what God has done. This is a story about God's grace transforming lost and hurting people.

congregation. Many of these young people had a connection with people from Golgota Budapest. In fact, some of Golgota's young men led Bible studies there. Szilárd Márkus, who had served as Golgota Budapest's assistant pastor since 1994, became a natural choice for the new church's senior pastor. Szilárd also oversees the homeless shelter.

Golgota Délpest. In 2009, Golgota Budapest continued to grow in numbers, and after a lot of prayer, we felt God calling us to start a new church on the east side of the city. God had raised up the right person to lead this new work, Laci Németh. Laci was originally from Subotica.

He had served as the assistant pastor in the southern Hungarian city of Szeged. He had also pastored a congregation in Croatia for several years. Then God led him to bring his family to the capital of Hungary to lead this new venture of faith.

Golgota Budapest determined to do a big outreach in that area of the city. We called this outreach "Lábnyom," which is the idea of a "footprint." In the book of Acts it says that everywhere Jesus placed His feet He did good. The idea is that wherever we go as Christians we should do good. And that became the theme of this outreach. In the outreach, the new congregation served the community by painting a preschool, offering sporting events to the neighborhood, and hosting children's games and music. The day culminated in a concert that included a gospel message. Out of this outreach, a new congregation was born.

Golgota 11. Then in 2011, as Golgota Budapest continued to grow, we decided to try another church plant. This time it would occur on the other side of the Danube River, the "Buda" side. We didn't see God raising up a pastor for this group, but we believed we needed to start something there and so we went back to prayer. For many months, we prayed about how we could reach more people in that part of Budapest.

As far as we know, a video-style church had not been tried in Eastern Europe. However, after praying, we felt God was calling us to take a chance. Just like we had learned from the very beginning of the ministry of Golgota, God wants us to take risks for Him. We prayed and then we brought it before the church. Most were excited about the thought of trying something different; some were skeptical. But all were curious to see what the Lord would do.

Because this church is located in the 11th district of Budapest, we call it Golgota 11. The church has its own worship teams and elders, but the Bible teaching is via video from the main campus. The response has overall been very good, and we are looking forward to how this could impact the rest of Budapest.

UNEXPECTED GRACE

From the end of the earth I call to You when my heart is faint. Lead me to the rock that is higher than I.

PSALM 61:2

By 2000, Golgota in Hungary was truly going through a transformation. That characteristic California style melded with a more typical Hungarian design as more and more of those who had come to Christ in the previous decade quite naturally took on roles of leadership. The couples leading congregations were no longer American imports but more often multicultural mixes—if not purely Hungarian.

Clearly this movement was proving itself to be bigger than some "American trend." From east to west, God was impacting souls in a way that transformed the course of their lives. And they would serve as His instruments to reach the next generation. But to raise up His chosen leaders in wisdom, God sometimes took them down roads none of us would choose to travel. Even the most difficult roads can be accentuated by unexpected grace.

CROSS-CULTURAL WEDDING

"To the bride and groom!" Everyone raised their glasses to honor Jeremy Ampe and his lovely Hungarian bride, Izabella. The crowd chattered in multiple languages as the music played at the reception hall in Kaposvár.

Árpi Horváth Kávai looked over at his wife, Angela. Eight months ago the cross-cultural wedding had been theirs. Angela leaned back in her chair and closed her eyes a moment. Clearly she was tired, but at three months pregnant, that is to be expected.

Árpi had become involved with Calvary Chapel while undergoing cancer treatments in Szeged many years before. He later attended Bible college at the Castle in Austria and now served as pastor in the beautiful college town of Pécs, Hungary.

"I guess it's time to go," Árpi smiled at his wife. He got up and gathered those who would be riding back with them.

It was only a little more than an hour's drive, but Angela already had begun to doze as soon as they left Kaposvár. Silence settled over the car as Árpi drove the road he knew so well.

Then suddenly, as he went around one curve, the car began to slide. It hit the guardrail and skidded along the side of it. Árpi gripped the steering wheel and struggled to get the vehicle under control, but it would not respond. They were sliding, and he could not get the car to stop.

There was a crash and chaos, glass and mangled metal, and when the dust settled, Angela lay bruised and broken, motionless. Árpi grabbed his phone with trembling hands and managed to call an ambulance. The longest minutes of his life followed. Finally, the ambulance arrived only to announce what Árpi feared most. His precious wife, the mother of his unborn child, was gone.

WHEN GOD DOESN'T MAKE SENSE

As news of Angela's death spread throughout the Golgota churches around the country, many were left wondering where God was in this tragedy. But none felt it as deeply as Árpi.

Back in Pécs, his friend, Jason VanderBurgh (a Kaposvár missionary), spent those first horrible weeks with him as he struggled to find a way to move forward.

Why? he would ask in his most desperate prayers. *What could be the purpose in this, Lord?*

There were times when the apartment door buzzer would ring, and he would half expect to find Angela standing there and the nightmare would be over. He wanted to believe it wasn't true. But then the cold absence in the bed beside him each night testified all too loudly that it was real.

"Why, Lord?" the question burned in his heart. There was no logic to it. He just ached. For a few weeks he did not preach on Sunday. He could not pretend like everything was all right, because everything was a disaster.

"Why would God do this?" he asked the unanswerable question to his closest friends. He did not really expect them to be able to make any sense of it. And they were wise enough not to try. Jason would reassuringly pat him on the back and pray with him. He did not let his friend walk this road alone.

At the end of all his painful questions, Árpi came to one conclusion. He would likely never know the "why" of this tragedy. But that really was not the issue. The bigger question was whether he would allow the unanswered questions to separate him from God.

Árpi concluded, *Do I know the answers? No. Would I like to? Yes! So will satisfying my intellect or curiosity be more important than following God? No.*

It was a conclusion that forced him forward in ministry and helping others, even though he might never understand the reason for his loss this side of heaven.

Árpi continued to serve and minister as the pastor of Golgota Pécs, but God would eventually call him to move on. And God had already begun crafting his replacement.

BACK IN BUDAPEST

Years earlier, a young man named Balázs Stanzel walked through the doors of Golgota Budapest wondering why he had come. If his friend had not called him right as he happened to be passing by, he would have never gone in.

He walked in and took a seat releasing a long irritated sigh. "Not another church," he said below his breath as he rolled his eyes. He crossed his arms and leaned back in the seat as he watched the praise team who led the singing. *Why is that girl smiling so much?*

Balázs really was not as hostile to God as it seemed. He did, however, feel hostile toward church. When he was 13 years old he had asked God to come into his life and be his Daddy, because he needed a father and his own was nowhere to be found. A loving, faithful grandfather had led him down the right path, but in high school he had drifted away, caught up in all the distractions of adolescence.

In his heart and mind he criticized every word that fell from Greg's mouth as Greg preached that day. And afterward, he marched up to talk to him, looking for a fight.

"Another church told me I'm probably demon possessed," he blurted out after introductions. Balázs had recently visited a highly charismatic church in the city, and they had come down on him hard.

Greg smiled at Balázs calmly. He didn't appear shocked or alarmed by the statement. He patted him on the shoulder and said, "Well, you're not possessed because I have the Holy Spirit living within me, and you wouldn't be calm around me if you had a demon inside you.

Greg's relaxed response surprised Balázs. And the fact that a pastor of such a large congregation would take the time to talk with him about these issues touched him deep inside. Balázs decided to return.

He would sneak in the back after worship and slip out quickly after the study. Some days he did not even listen to Greg. He would just spend the forty minutes reading his Bible. Over the course of the next nine months, God awakened Balázs to what a relationship with Him could really mean. Finally, at a service in 2003, he became overwhelmed with the sense that God was calling him to do something really significant. He went forward and prayed, *Oh God, show me Your miracles! I want to know You—You make sense of my life!*

MAKING SENSE OF THE SENSELESS

Enjoying much success in his work in audio and video production, Balázs was working a big Formula One World Championship video project a month after he committed himself to the Lord. One day he suddenly collapsed. The medical exams came back with terrible news: He had testicular cancer.

Balázs had dealt with such health problems before. He knew the ropes. Sick leave, extended treatment, and then move on.

"So how much sick leave should I schedule to take?" he asked the doctor calmly.

The doctor looked at him incredulously. "I do not think you understand," he responded, as his eyes grew intense. "You might not make it three weeks. That is how bad it is."

A chill of fear rippled through Balázs as his jaw dropped. He suddenly realized he might not make it through this first surgery. The young videographer went home and grabbed his Bible. He began reading through the book of John looking for comfort.

He read the Scriptures aloud. And something happened. Although he had read these same words many times since childhood, and he knew many Bible verses by heart, now as he read it, something was so different. It was as if Jesus stood right there with him whispering words of comfort into his ears. Eventually he got to John 14:27 where he read, "Peace I leave with you; My peace I give to you. Not as the world gives do I give to you. Let not your hearts be troubled, neither let them be afraid."

The words filled his fearful heart with comfort and an inexplicable peace. It was something he could scarcely hope to explain. But he called his brother, overwhelmed with what was happening.

"Hello, Barni?" Balázs clenched his Bible close to his heart with one arm and gripped the phone with the other. "You won't believe this! They just told me I have cancer. They just told me I might not make it three weeks. I'm scheduled for an operation tomorrow and I have the biggest peace I've ever had in my life—ever."

It did not make any sense. He had made it in the competitive world of TV production. He had run the giant screens for the biggest shows. At 20 years old, he earned a ridiculously large salary. But in all that success, he had never experienced the kind of peace he did right at this moment as he stared death in the face.

THE TOUGH ROAD

Anyone who has ever been through cancer treatment knows that even in the best cases, it's a tough road. But Balázs knew he wasn't alone. He chose not to get all wrapped up in the questions of why, but instead to saturate himself in all the Scriptures that talked about peace.

He started cancer treatments in September and by November he had endured six rounds of heavy chemo. His body began wasting away to nothing, as food was no longer an option. He lost about sixty-five pounds, which was almost half his body weight. Like a skeleton draped in a thin layer of skin, he lay in a hospital bed, wondering how long he could hold on.

In the oncology ward, he quickly learned that this was not the place to make friends. He would politely say hello to the guys in the other beds, but it had to end there. Every day someone would leave the ward with a sheet pulled over his face. By Christmas, Balázs wondered if he too would soon make that journey. His liver started failing. In fact, it stopped working twice before New Years, requiring an emergency blood transfusion.

SUFFERING IN PEACE

"Just hold on Balázs," the nurse said to him as he felt himself slipping away. "The blood is coming." The hard-nosed Hungarian nurse looked at him with tears welling up in her eyes as she prepped him for the transfusion.

Balázs nodded, his face gray with lifelessness. He knew she had seen death before, and he wondered why she would shed tears for him. He let his mind fall back into the Scriptures: "And the peace of God, which surpasses all understanding, will guard your hearts..." He sensed something supernatural in that hospital ward. It wasn't something he could see with his eyes, but it felt almost tangible to his spirit. He thought to himself, *There is so clearly a God who reigns over all this in peace.*

BAD NEWS

By February, doctors hoped the chemo would have knocked out all the secondary tumors. But when they ran the tests, they discovered the tumors had doubled in size and number. Had Balázs endured all this just to die in the end?

"Peace I leave with you; My peace I give to you. Not as the world gives do I give to you. Let not your hearts be troubled, neither let them be afraid." Balázs held on to the Scriptures that had given him hope from the beginning.

Balázs had one last option, a major surgery. And he would likely not even make it off the operating table. The only other option was to sit back and wait to die. He took a deep breath and agreed to go forward with it. He called his pastor the night before the surgery.

"Hello, Greg?" Balázs' boney fingers clenched the phone. "I just wanted to say, thanks. Thank you for everything." He laughed a sober laugh at the awkwardness of the call. "This is crazy." He then regained his serious tone. "I'll see you in heaven."

Balázs hung up the phone and let out a deep breath. Whatever happened, whatever his future held, be it heaven or earth, he was at peace.

But Greg was not ready to give up so easily. He had joined a 24-hour prayer chain, organized by some Campus Crusade friends, dedicated to praying for Balázs' healing.

And they prayed and prayed. God heard those prayers and chose to breathe life into his dying body.

MOVING ON

Balázs survived the surgery, but he was not out of the woods yet. Only time would tell if all the tumors were really gone. In the meantime, as Balázs began to regain strength and become more mobile, Greg had some ideas for the young miracle in the making.

"Hey Balázs, why don't you come help with the outreach we're doing this weekend?"

"I don't know. I'm still kind of weak," Balázs answered.

"Come on," Greg insisted. "It would be so awesome if you could share what the Lord has done for you. We'll make it as easy on you as possible."

Balázs agreed. And soon he was sitting with an American girl named Leah Tucker preparing to speak to a crowd about Jesus. Leah was a Bible college student originally from San Luis Obispo, California. Balázs was immediately taken with the peace she walked in and the passion she served with. When he learned she was a cancer survivor as well, he knew she understood the peace he had experienced. Because of this shared bond, he felt connected to her on a deeper level. Their stories of battles with cancer and the peace of Jesus made them a natural team, and they were asked to speak together at additional events. And weeks later when Balázs' tests came back miraculously clear of all cancer, he knew he wanted to marry this girl.

But before the wedding bells, Balázs headed off to the Bible college. The head knowledge he gained there resonated with the heart knowledge he possessed because of his experiences. His heart burned with a passion for Christ because of what He had done for him and because of what He had brought him through. Indeed, his God had proven Himself to be a God of miracles.

Balázs sharing

FINDING A PLACE IN MINISTRY

After finishing Bible college, Leah and Balázs were married, and the time had come to find a place of ministry. They visited a number of different cities. They were open to anything. Well, almost anything. Balázs drew the line at serving as pastor. The thought of standing up in front of a group and teaching was a little terrifying to him.

As they explored the possibilities, Balázs spoke with his friend Árpi.

"What would you say about Leah and I coming to Pécs?"

"I really need a Timothy," Árpi answered honestly. "But I really can't be a Paul." Balázs understood what he meant. Árpi had been through a great deal. And although he had truly come through the wilderness of his tragedy and moved forward in ministry and life, he was tired. It had been five years since that horrible night of Angela's death. Since that time, he pushed forward with the work of pastoring the small congregation in Pécs. As the years passed, God led Árpi to marry an accomplished Hungarian woman, Andrea Németh, who had come to Christ in Subotica years earlier in the days when Mike Harris preached on the streets. She had served as Greg's translator in Budapest for many years. Andrea understood Árpi's loss intimately, because it had been her loss too. Angela had been her dear friend.

With all the pressures of the pastoring, Árpi was just exhausted. He could not be all he would like to be, and he wanted to make sure Balázs understood that. Balázs and Leah came ready to serve in any way they could, from setting up chairs for services to leading music.

For years, Árpi had a vision for several different outreaches for the church. First, he really wanted to see the church get involved with orphans. Secondly, he believed the congregation should try to reach the youth in prison. And since Pécs was a college town, he thought they should naturally be ministering to students. But despite years of prayer, God had not yet opened the doors.

Balázs and Leah shared this vision in every way. They had not called the town home more than a few weeks when things started happening. Not long after they moved there, a student fellowship began in their home.

Balázs headed over to the employment office, as he would need a job to help support he and his wife. He chatted with a guy from the Pentecostal church, sharing his vision to work with youth in prisons. Of course, he did not really know how that would happen since there were no youth prisons in Pécs.

"Actually," the man told Balázs, "the federal prison just opened a whole youth wing last week. If you have time, I can introduce you to the pastor who oversees the prison work. Maybe you can work with him until you get a job."

So Balázs went and met with the prison pastor. He carried a letter of recommendation from Golgota, not knowing if that name would hold any credibility with a Reformed church cleric.

Balázs introduced himself and explained his vision and desire to reach out to the troubled youth behind bars.

The pastor eyed the letter and looked back at Balázs. "My son and his family live in Florida," the pastor said. "They attend a Calvary Chapel there and have told me many great things about it."

Balázs smiled. "I believe God can do great things right here as well," he said.

Typically it takes about six months to get the bureaucratic approval to begin ministering in the prisons, but because God had orchestrated His favor upon Balázs, he had the necessary credentials in just twenty-eight days.

LOOKING TO THE FUTURE

As Balázs and Leah settled into marriage, the question of children arose. Having been brought to the brink of death due to testicular cancer, Balázs' chances of being able to father a child were not high. But that did not bother Leah. She always had a heart for children and orphans, and becoming a mother through adoption was just as good as far as she was concerned.

But if God really was a God of miracles, why couldn't they trust Him for a child? The issue weighed heavily on Balázs' heart.

"Leah, what if we tried to have a baby. I mean biologically." He posed the question to his wife one day.

Leah's eyebrows rose at the idea. She sat down beside her husband and wrapped her arms around him. "You know, I'm totally okay with adoption, right?"

"Yeah, yeah, I know," he said. "It's just that I've been really feeling like maybe God wants us to have a biological child too." Balázs kissed his wife. "You know it wouldn't be the first miracle God ever did."

Balázs traveled to the medical center at Székesfehérvár to be thoroughly checked out. After a day of being poked and prodded by needles and machines, the doctor came out to talk with him.

"Given your medical history, there's no way you should be able to have kids," the doctor said as he shook his head.

The statement did not shock Balázs. He didn't expect the doctor to say much else. But the doctor continued.

"However, as I look at the results of your tests, well, I can't really say that you absolutely cannot have kids."

Balázs' lips parted into a big smile as the doctor explained how he should take a series of vitamins to boost his cells to improve his chances. The couple ordered them immediately from the States. Balázs and Leah beamed with expectation. Maybe God really would do a miracle.

But that miracle would have to be two-sided. Although Leah no longer had brain cancer she still suffered from periodic seizures. And having a baby while suffering seizures is a difficult mix. This pregnancy would have to be saturated in prayer.

Much to their surprise, Leah found out she was pregnant even before the vitamin supplements arrived. They were both overjoyed with the news, but they paid close attention to Leah's health. Day after day they prayed, watched and waited as the tiny baby grew inside her. Miraculously, from the time she got pregnant, all seizures ceased. Experiencing blessing upon blessing and miracle upon miracle, their baby girl was born on November 25, 2006.

In time they would have other children and adopt as well. Their home would have no shortage of childhood giggles and butterfly kisses.

A CHANGE OF HEART

Almost immediately after settling in Pécs, something started to change in Balázs' heart. He felt so deeply intertwined with this congregation. He would come home from prayer meetings in tears because he ached with those who ached.

What's wrong with me? He would ask himself. *I shouldn't feel like this. I am not the pastor!*

But he could not ignore it; a pastor's heart was burning inside

Balázs, Leah, and their children

him. It was not something he looked for or even wanted. But it was something God chose to place within him.

Soon the fateful day came when Árpi had a talk with Balázs.

"Balázs, Andrea and I feel like God is calling us to move on," Árpi said. "I was wondering if you'd pray about taking over the church as pastor."

Suddenly it all made sense. As much as he did not want to be the guy up there teaching, God had called him to it. God had placed a pastor's heart inside him.

And so that bitter child from the village became a man filled with peace and love. That kid who hated church became the pastor of Golgota Pécs. And that man who should not even be alive or have kids had a home full of little ones. That is Balázs' story.

LOVE AND GRACE

Not far from Pécs, in the city of Kaposvár, God was writing another story of unexpected grace. (Names have been changed to protect the identity of those involved.) Steve had come to work with us in 1999, and it was not long before a lovely, godly young woman caught his eye. Júlia's sweet spirit and gentle manner mesmerized the wild and crazy American. And since she didn't really speak English, he quickly became a man on a lingual mission. I had never seen someone learn Hungarian so fast. Steve was in love, and in the summer of 2001, they married, adding to the ever-growing list of cross-cultural couples ministering in Hungary.

Steve and Júlia were a spiritual "dream team." They ministered side by side both in Kaposvár and in the new congregation planted in a nearby village. Steve had ministered in the refugee camp there for years, and that ministry had spilled over into the surrounding village. God was truly doing amazing things both in the ministry and in their personal lives as Júlia soon gave birth to their son, Jonathan.

Babies bring adjustments. And these adjustments would not come easily to this couple. Steve had enjoyed having his wife working with him, by his side. Ministering together bound them as they shared a vision and a passion for the work of God.

But now it had all been interrupted. Steve found himself without his best friend, partner, and helpmate as he made the forty-minute drive to the village each day. Júlia stayed home, overwhelmed with all the responsibilities and sleeplessness that come with a newborn baby. And their lives began to grow in different directions.

DRIFTING APART

Keep your heart with all vigilance, for from it flow the springs of life. (Proverbs 4:23)

"I'm home," Steve announced when he got back one day.

"Shhhh! Quiet!" Júlia sharply responded. The dark circles of sleeplessness surrounded her eyes. "Jonathan is finally asleep."

Steve sat down on the couch and sighed. He wanted to talk about the good things God was doing. Júlia just wanted to get a few minutes of rest before the baby woke up again.

What's wrong with her? Steve grumbled to himself. *I guess she really isn't as spiritual as I used to think.*

Steve continued his pilgrimages to the village each week. Sometimes young people from the Kaposvár church would come to help. Steve welcomed the company. It was good to have someone to share the ministry with, especially since his wife was now occupied with the baby.

Steve enjoyed the young people. They admired him, and their presence made the trip a little less lonely. One young woman in particular seemed to really share his passion for ministering. She became a close friend, someone with whom he could share his frustrations and trials. And she seemed so spiritually in tune with him. He admired her spiritual insight. In fact, he found himself admiring a lot more about her as time passed.

Steve tried to dismiss the emotional attachment as just a kind of spiritual camaraderie, but he found his mind drifting into thoughts about her often. *This has to stop*, he would say to himself. And then he would remember how she had encouraged him earlier that day. And he would sit back and smile as he thought of her.

Maybe if I confess my feelings to her, then we'll be able to keep the proper distance, he reasoned to himself. *Honesty is always the best way.* He then determined to get it out in the open, at least out in the open between the two of them privately.

"Listen," he said to her one night as they returned from doing a Bible study. "We've become such close friends that I..." he hesitated a moment. "Well, I am starting to have feelings for you, and I shouldn't because I'm married."

The young girl smiled up at him. Flattered that the dynamic young American would find her attractive, she giggled a little. "Yes, you're right," she agreed. "It's wrong, but I have to admit I have feelings for you too."

Steve felt a certain fleshly satisfaction in knowing his affections were returned. But it was immoral, and he could never act on those feelings. So he committed to tell no one else of his struggle and made no changes in what had become a precarious situation for his marriage.

The battle continued. His spirit knew it was wrong, but his flesh so enjoyed her company and her support. *It was not as if they had sinned,* he reasoned as he gave himself permission to let the emotional attachment continue.

The path he traveled proved to be a predictable one. As time passed, he confided more and more in his "friend." The emotional attachment grew stronger and eventually erupted into physical sin.

IN THE AFTERMATH

Steve stood in front of the apartment building he called home. He could see the light on where Júlia was likely rocking their son to sleep. Tears welled up in his eyes as he gathered up the courage to do what must be done. He took a deep breath and got control of himself. *Will she be able to forgive me?* He wondered. *Will she even want to try?*

Steve forced himself to swallow the big knot in his throat and headed inside.

"Júlia, I need to talk to you," he said, his voice almost trembling.

She put the baby in his crib and returned, sensing that this was something serious. "What is it?" she asked cautiously.

"I, I don't know how to say this," he stammered. "I guess I should just come out with it." He shuffled around trying to come up with the right words. "It's just that, well, you know I've been feeling so far from you… and then there was this girl... and she was always there... and, and..." He paused and looked at his wife with tears running down his face. "I sinned. I totally blew it! I'm so sorry."

So overwhelmed by his own sin and shame, he could scarcely look his wife in the face.

Júlia's eyes now swam in her own tears. She reached out and hugged her husband. "I don't want our marriage to end," she sobbed.

They cried together, and as they began to regain control, they took a hard look at where their marriage had gone wrong, and what it would take to fix it.

"Maybe we need to go to the States for a while, get away from here and start over," Júlia suggested.

RADICAL CHANGES

Within two weeks, they were on a plane to Steve's home in California. In the back of their minds they thought they would get some counseling and be back to Hungary in six months. But a marriage so broken cannot be quickly repaired. God held them, half a world away from where their marriage fell apart, for five full years.

Steve and Júlia rediscovered each other, learned how to communicate, and fell head over heels in love again. In time, they let go of the idea of returning to Hungary. At times, Steve would remember the good old days back in his wife's homeland, the days when they ministered together and watched God do awesome things. And his heart would ache at how cavalierly he had thrown it all away. *If I were God, I'd never use me again,* he thought to himself.

And yet, after some time, God did use him in various ministries in California. From leading Bible studies to working with children, they had grown so content in the place where God had brought them that after the first three or four years, they no longer had any intention of returning to Hungary. But God's grace can come unexpectedly.

NEW VISION

"Hey Steve, Júlia! Merry Christmas!" Joy and I greeted the couple when we were back in California for Christmas in 2009. We met them for lunch at a local restaurant. As we sat down at the table and chatted, I could see in this couple such a story of restoration, a story of grace.

"So when are you guys moving back to Hungary?" I asked with a smile. I wanted him to know that God's forgiveness is so complete that if God decided to call them back, we would welcome them with open arms.

"Well, I don't know," Steve looked at his wife, clearly taken aback by the question. The truth was that they had no intention of moving back. They loved Hungary, but they had also let go of the dream, the vision they once had of ministering there. "Um, well, we'll be on the short-term team coming in the summer," he explained.

We talked about the upcoming trip and reminisced about the good times we had had together in Hungary.

That week a local church sponsored a conference, and Steve and Júlia decided to go. The conference renewed that passion for missions that had always burned in their souls. On the way home from the conference, Steve turned to Júlia and said, "They say there's a need at the Golgota in northern

Hungary. What if we checked it out while we're in the country this summer?"

Júlia smiled at the idea of returning to her homeland. "Let's start praying about it," she said.

Steve and Júlia visited the city to consider whether the Lord might want to use them there. It felt good to be back in Hungary. All the good memories rushed into their souls as they met people and imagined what living and ministering in this Hungarian city. And as much as it was familiar, this new city held a freshness, a difference from the part of Hungary where they began so many years before. Maybe God really could redeem their ministry as completely as He had their marriage.

The following year on July 15, exactly twelve years to the day from when Steve first arrived in Hungary, they returned to plant a new church. They knew that despite the shame of sin, their story testifies that the grace of God is strong enough to save and restore the most broken of souls.

GRACE BEYOND THE BORDERS

"But you will receive power when the Holy Spirit has come upon you, and you will be My witnesses in Jerusalem and in all Judea and Samaria, and to the end of the earth."

ACTS 1:8

Barbaric. Argaw Ayele looked at his brother's wounds of war. When the Ethiopian government had called for soldiers to fight in the war against Eritrea, a small country bordering Ethiopia, his brother had answered and fought. He had suffered irreparable damage in the crossfire. Now left maimed for his sacrifice, the government no longer wanted anything to do with him. Argaw felt sickened by it, sickened by a nation that would use its people and then toss them aside like garbage when they were no longer of use. It was nothing short of barbaric.

He would not live in such a nation, he determined. He contacted a friend in Ukraine and managed to work out a yearlong student visa. All that mattered was that he was getting out of Ethiopia.

A PLAN OF ESCAPE

Argaw knew the student visa served only as a temporary fix. He would be forced back to Ethiopia if he could not orchestrate something within the twelve-month time frame. For five months he tried to secure visas to different nations. But again and again, the various bureaucracies hit him with rejection.

Running out of options, he grew desperate. He could not get sent back. He would not let that happen. The thought of his maimed brother haunted him, angered him. He would do anything to avoid having to return there.

There seemed to be only one option left. If he could not do it legally, then he would defy the law. Soon he found himself surrounded by dark, unsavory characters that specialized in organized crime. Expert smugglers, their goods were neither drugs nor hard liquor. These abusive brutes capitalized on desperation—trafficking human lives.

Through various avenues and friends of friends, Argaw arranged to meet with one in a seedy location one night.

"So you want to be moved into Western Europe?" the large man asked.

"I can't go back to Ethiopia. I'll do anything," Argaw pleaded.

The man almost smiled through his stained teeth. "It'll cost you $1,000 paid up front."

"Okay, I'll get it. You just have to get me out of here before they deport me." Argaw began to utilize every means he had to get the funds together.

HARSH JOURNEY

But Argaw's trip to a new life proved to be more than he bargained for.

"Get in the trunk," the large man commanded, as he opened it.

"What?" Argaw asked, confused. The man grabbed him by the shoulder and threw him in the compartment. "Hey! What are you doing?" Argaw protested.

"What's the matter? Did you think you were traveling first class?" the man said, laughing at his little joke as he slammed the trunk shut.

In the darkness, Argaw's body flung from side-to-side as his transporters raced down rough, curvy roads at unconscionable speeds. When the trunk finally opened, he felt sick and bruised. But the abusive journey had only begun. They pulled him from the trunk, and an icy gust of wind hit Argaw in the face. He shivered. An African could never be prepared to endure a Ukrainian winter, even in the best of cases. And this was clearly not the best of cases.

"Across the river you will find an old, abandoned house," One of the smugglers barked as he shoved Argaw. "Stay there until someone comes for you."

"How am I supposed to cross the river?" Argaw asked, as a few flurries blew by on the wind.

"Take that raft," one of them grumbled. The "raft" was really just some sort of inflated animal skin. They set the poor African afloat, leaving him in the middle of nowhere—in Ukraine, in winter—to freeze in a tiny house with no heat.

SEEKING ASYLUM

After a month of harsh treatment and travel, Argaw was dropped off in front of the refugee camp in Bicske, Hungary, not far from Budapest.

"There's the refugee camp," one smuggler pointed to a fenced area full of dreary gray buildings. "You need to seek asylum."

Argaw walked up to the front door and took a deep breath. It wasn't pretty, but at least it was not Ethiopia. It would just be the first step to the rest of his life, one without war and torture, a future of hope.

Although the camp's accommodations were hardly luxurious, they did meet his basic needs. And within those walls, he found friends in a number of people from Ethiopia, as well as the missionaries who came to bring the message of Christ.

Argaw had no intention of staying in Hungary. He planned to go to England and had begun the paperwork to appeal for acceptance there as an immigrant. But that process does not occur overnight. While he waited, he often met with the missionaries. Through them, all the stories from God's Word that he had learned from childhood came alive, and he rediscovered his Savior.

LEFT BEHIND

In time, the other Ethiopian refugees won official "refugee" status and moved on to build new lives in various countries. But Argaw found himself completely alone. He was drowning in a sea of people from what seemed like every culture of the world—except his own.

"God, I'm so confused," he cried out. "I don't know what to do! You've found all my friends here a place. Why not me?"

The answer would not come quickly. So Argaw did the only productive thing he could do: live one day at a time and get to know God better.

He studied the Word with the missionaries and found himself completely fascinated by it. He could hardly wait until the next study. And so in this place of waiting, Argaw grew in the ways of the Lord.

Although he had applied for Hungarian residency and a work permit, he had been denied on both counts. These rejections piled up on a host of others. But there was one place where he would not find rejection. When he took the train to Golgota Budapest on Sundays, he found a place that gave him a little sense of home. In time, the church grew to love Argaw as much as Argaw loved the church. And in the young Ethiopian, Greg Opean saw potential for something great.

"Have you ever thought about going to Bible college?" Greg asked.

"I don't know," Argaw said. He really hadn't thought about it, but he knew he loved studying the Word.

"We can make it happen," Greg encouraged.

"That would be great!" Argaw smiled at the thought. It enticed him. At the refugee camp, his life was stalled. If he could go to Bible college, he would really feel like he was finally moving forward.

A HEART FOR ETHIOPIA

Of course, the lifestyle of Bible college proved quite different from the culture of the refugee camp. Adjustments took time, but before long Argaw found himself pursuing God in new ways, which naturally meant he would be changed.

Bible college brimmed with bright-eyed idealistic students from a variety of backgrounds. Some were Hungarians, like Tamás Gémes and Balázs Stanzel, who would one day pastor churches in Hungary. Others were Americans, who had a heart to reach the world for Christ.

One day, in the midst of a crowded room of meandering students, a young American girl marched up to Argaw.

"Hi, I'm Rachel, and you're Argaw," the young woman said. "I want to go to Ethiopia."

Taken aback a little by the young lady's directness, Argaw responded, "Why don't we talk when it's not so crowded?"

Rachel shrugged her shoulders and said, "Okay." And then she disappeared into the crowd. But she would be back.

Rachel harbored an inexplicable passion for Ethiopia since she was a child. When she was 15, her youth group leader had them do an exercise where they wrote down three things they would like to do in their lives. He claimed writing it down increased the chances of it actually happening. For Rachel it had been a simple exercise. She wrote that she'd like to be a missionary in Ethiopia, be a doctor in Ethiopia, and lead worship in Ethiopia.

When she decided to study at the Bible college in Hungary, she could hardly believe it when she saw Ethiopia on the list of countries the Bible college had sent short-term teams to. She felt as if all her life culminated in this opportunity to actually serve on a short-term missions trip to the land she loved.

TELL ME YOUR VISION

Envoys will come out of Egypt; Ethiopia will quickly stretch out her hands to God. (Psalm 68:31–NKJV)

Sitting at the college coffee bar one day, Argaw caught a glimpse of the eager young American. He motioned for her to come over. She almost ran.

Argaw looked at the bright-eyed American. She could have no idea what his home country was really like. "Tell me your vision for Ethiopia," he said gently, "and I'll tell you mine."

Words began pouring from Rachel's mouth almost before she could think. "Well, I don't so much have a specific vision, but I know I love Ethiopia and I know I have to go there. I've known since I was 15, probably before that. And I want to help the poor and orphans. They suffer so much there." Rachel's eyes clouded with tears as she thought of those poor helpless souls.

Argaw sensed such a genuine compassion in this girl's heart for a place she had never been, a place she could not begin to understand. He smiled slightly at her.

"Let me tell you my vision," Argaw said as he began to explain in detail how things worked in Ethiopia and how he hoped to help the people there. As he spoke, Rachel could scarcely listen. God was moving in her heart in a way she had never experienced before—and never has since. It was as if God Himself stood there and imparted to her some knowledge of her future. She knew she would marry this man and minister in Ethiopia by his side.

REALIGNING VISIONS

At first, Argaw had no interest in doing more than short-term mission trips to the nation that had hurt him so deeply. But after he led the first team, he began to believe God was calling him to go back and bring hope to this hopeless society.

"But it's impossible, God," he prayed. "I couldn't go back and live in Ethiopia if I wanted to. And I don't want to."

Argaw had no money, and there were no established ministries to plug in to. Even if he managed to work out those obstacles, he legally could not return. No, it was not an option. But God kept pressing him.

He tried to negotiate with God. "I'll go anywhere to serve you, Lord, but please—not Ethiopia."

As Argaw struggled with this issue, his relationship with Rachel grew. How could he not love a woman so eager to leave the wealth of America to bring comfort to his suffering nation? She seemed to love his people more than he did. That was convicting. Maybe with her by his side, he could go back. If God could work out all the impossibilities, he finally conceded to God that he would go.

And so the God of miracles made the impossible possible yet again.

IN ETHIOPIA

Two years later, from a Bible college in Hungary, the newly wed couple set out for Africa. In the next few years they would establish the Ebenezer Grace Children's Home, providing hope and care for thirty-two children, from 5 months old to 11 years of age. They support poverty stricken families and help kids who cannot afford to go to school. Teaching Bible studies to the young and old, Argaw and Rachel continued to be God's instruments to bring His miracles to a devastated land.

Argaw, Rachel, and their children

Ebenezer Grace Children's Home

UNLIKELY TOOLS

Argaw was not the only tool God would funnel through Hungary to reach the world. God finds His chosen tools in the most unexpected places.

"Bang! Bang!" The Nigerian pounded on the door of the Budapest apartment where a man known as the "Passport Handler" resided. "You must help me!" the Nigerian cried.

"Go away!" the Passport Handler shouted back.

"You've received money to help me!" Prince Lawrence, the African insisted. "You took my passport! Where am I supposed to go?"

A large, surly man opened the door and pushed the Nigerian back, almost off his feet. "Keep your voice down," he snarled. "And go away. I don't want to see you now."

"How am I supposed to get to Holland?" Prince pleaded.

"That's not my problem," the Handler said as he slammed the door shut.

Feeling desperate, Prince left, but not for long. When he returned later, the Handler was gone, along with the money.

Prince Lawrence, a reporter by trade, had written a few too many articles from the "wrong" perspective, as far as the Nigerian government was concerned. As a result, he had a choice. He could stay in his homeland and risk abuse and imprisonment, or he could run. He chose to run.

His plan had been to settle in either Holland or Italy. Both had a reputation for being more open to Africans and both had stellar reputations for their football (soccer) teams, a sport he loved. Unfortunately, due to his unscrupulous "handler," both remained out of his reach.

However, what Prince never suspected was that God was orchestrating a much larger plan than he could have ever imagined or conceived.

FRANTIC ACTIONS

Frantic and fearful, Prince climbed aboard a train to Debrecen without even a passport and hoped something would happen. Something did. Prince was arrested and sent to a remote refugee camp in Nyírbátor, which operated much like a prison. For twenty-one days, he suffered interrogation and investigations into his reasons for fleeing his homeland.

From there he was sent to a refugee camp in Debrecen. At the camp, there was a young American woman named Rosemary who came and invited refugees to church. Remembering the faith he had been taught since childhood, and needing a sense of hope, Prince decided to go.

The church didn't meet in a fancy building with stained-glass windows and statues. No, the humble congregation met in a cellar room not far from downtown. As Bodi, the doctor-turned-pastor began teaching from the Word of God, something struck Prince. Every word resonated in the deepest parts of his soul. The Word was truly "living and active, sharper than any two-edged sword."

After thirty minutes, Prince sat back in awe—not of Bodi's extraordinary eloquence, but rather at the beautiful, simplistic manner in which the Word was taught.

Why hasn't anyone explained the Bible to us in Nigeria like this before? he wondered.

After that Sunday, Prince could not get the experience out of his head. He wanted his people to know and experience God's Word in this way. Between playing pick-up soccer at the camp and eating his meager meals, Prince's mind would often wander back to Nigeria. He remembered his aging parents, and his soul was stirred by thoughts of them going to meet the Savior before learning to know Him in this way.

REFUGEE CAMP SHAKE UP

The 9/11 tragedy in America shook the world, and tremors even reached the refugee system in Hungary. Suddenly, Prince and the other African refugees were moved to the Bicske Camp, which is located just outside Budapest. Authorities needed to make space at Debrecen, a more remote location, for Middle Eastern refugees.

The change proved to be a great blessing to Prince, who quickly became involved in Golgota Budapest. Each week, Prince could not wait for Sunday morning to roll around. The studies and the fellowship were like living water to his parched soul. And within those walls, Prince found himself awakened to new heights and understanding of what a relationship with God could be.

The Nigerian loved Greg's casual style of teaching. Greg used humor and everyday illustrations that connected the ancient Scriptures to real life. As a result, the Word of God came alive in Prince's heart in ways it never had before, and others noticed.

"Hey Prince," someone at church stopped him one day. "I believe God's going to use you in full-time ministry some day."

The thought appealed to the young Nigerian, but it was probably wishful thinking more than anything else. After all, he was not the boisterous, dynamic preacher-type. In fact, he was so timid and shy that there were times as a child his dad would have to spank Prince just to get him to talk. *While I would love to serve the Lord, full-time ministry isn't for me,* Prince thought.

But God's people were willing to take a chance on this man. Soon he was enrolled in Bible college, even though he had no interest in becoming a pastor or missionary. As he studied the Scriptures at the Bible college in Vajta, God began an even deeper work in his heart.

If only the Nigerian people could learn how to study the Word like this, Prince thought. His soul ached for the people of his homeland. He knew what God was doing. God had allowed him to come here to learn. Who better to take the Word to Nigeria than a Nigerian?

But Prince resisted. *I can't go, Lord,* he prayed. *What would they do to me if I returned?* Haunted by fear, yet pursued by the Spirit of God, Prince struggled for three months. He hardly slept. He attended classes by day, but all the while God's call on his life was tugging.

Lord, I managed to get out of that place, he prayed. *Do You know how many people are trying to get out?* Of course, he knew God did. *I'd be crazy to return. I don't understand what You're doing here.*

God placed a verse on his heart. "A man's steps are from the LORD; how then can man understand his way?"

Prince continued to wrestle with God until that fateful day he gave in. *If You make a way, Lord, I'll go.*

STEP OF FAITH

By that time, Prince had finished Bible college, and his internship was almost over. He made a phone call to Nigeria to see if his country would even take him back. He was shocked to discover that the nation had cleared him of all charges, and the door to return was open.

During Argaw and Prince's internships at the Bible college, it was evident the Lord's hand was upon their lives. I had promised if they ever had the opportunity to go back to their home countries, that I would go with them. By God's grace I was able to accompany them both.

The trip to Ethiopia was fruitful. During that first trip the Lord gave Argaw a vision to start an orphanage. He was to impact whomever the Lord brought onto his path with the Word of God.

On our trip to Nigeria, we took a small team with the purpose of helping Prince begin a new church in the capital city of Abuja. In those two weeks, we were able to preach the gospel in schools and on the streets. Since day one, Prince has served as senior pastor and out of this first church plant, four other churches in Nigeria began. God called a timid man to be a leader of many, but his days of trials had just begun.

TIMES OF TRIAL

"Blessed are you when others revile you and persecute you and utter all kinds of evil against you falsely on My account." (Matthew 5:11)

A land of opposites, Nigeria serves as a home for both extreme affluence and severe poverty. In the minds of many there, human life holds little value. Like many of the nations of Africa, the threat of war is always on the horizon. Presently, Christians are being persecuted in Nigeria on a horrific scale. Hundreds have been killed in just the last few years.

Prince experienced Nigeria's sinister side in what began as a normal Friday evening. He and his wife, Florence, had recently moved and were hosting some friends. Prince went to the back of the building to turn on the power generator, not knowing that some unwanted guests were lurking in the dark. As soon as the generator began rumbling, the criminals knew that no one would be able to hear the screams.

Prince, Florence, and their children

Forcing their way into the apartment, the attackers demanded that everyone lie face down, even the two women who were both pregnant. They punched Prince in the face and roughed him up before hitting him in the head with the butt of a gun.

While Prince was unconscious, they locked his wife and friends in the bathroom. They ransacked and looted everything of worth—laptops, an MP3 player, Prince's sermon record containing many messages from the church, money, watches, jewelry, and mobile phones.

They grabbed his wife and threatened her. "Tell us where you keep the money!" they demanded. But there was no hidden money.

Then they revived Prince. "Where's the money?" they snarled.

"I'm a teacher of the Bible," he explained. "I am not a businessman!"

At that point one of them asked, "So, you're a pastor?"

Prince answered, "Yes."

"Of which church?" The man eyed him as he waited for a response.

"Calvary Chapel, over at SSS Quarters Extension," Prince replied. The revelation seemed to shock them and make them think for a moment about what they were doing. But it was not enough to make them leave.

The assailants threw them all back into the bathroom, and the scared group sang worship songs and prayed for their captors, for their souls and for their salvation. Finally, when they felt convinced the thieves had left, they broke the bathroom door down and freed themselves.

Prince called the police, but they told him they would not come unless he agreed to pay for their fuel to get there. Prince sighed as he heard the policeman's conditions. He realized that their safety and well-being did not depend on the police. The Lord would be their shield and on Him they would rely.

Prince and his family sorted out the remnants of their pillaged apartment and tried to piece their lives together. Life went forward.

Two Sundays later, as Prince taught at the church, he looked out over the congregation and saw one of the robbers sitting in the service, waiting to hear a message of grace. Prince made a point to go to him and greet him with a smile.

God has given Prince tremendous "staying grace" as he seeks to serve in such a volatile environment. The pressure to quit and leave is always present. But intermingled among the regular bouts of malaria, deaths in the family, and Islamic extremism, Calvary Chapel Abuja has remained a beacon of light in the nation of Nigeria.

TO THE ENDS OF THE EARTH

From America to Europe to Africa, the reach of God's grace knows no bounds. His love is being poured out on the nations—even as far as Asia.

Paul Billings wiped the sweat from his brow after loading the last of his and his wife's baggage on the train. Besides all the bags of food, clothes, and toiletries, he dragged the accordion, the saxophone, and the guitar into their compartment. Having a wife who loved music, he was just thankful he did not have to carry a piano. Transferring trains with this load in the busy Moscow train station had been a nightmare. If it were not for the blessing of a missionary contact that had helped them, Paul did not know how they would have done it. But now they were settled in, as the train started rattling down the track again. A few more days of travel and they would finally be in Bishkek, Kyrgyzstan. It hardly seemed real.

It seemed like it had been forever since they had left his in-laws' home in Kiev, Ukraine the previous day. His wife Melanie, although an American, had largely grown up in Ukraine. Her parents, George and Pam Markey, were longtime missionaries and experienced people of faith. Their history of bringing the gospel to Ukraine in the volatile post-communist era was the stuff of legends. Paul had enjoyed the time he had spent with them. But now it was time for him and Melanie to begin a new chapter of God's story of grace to the nation of Kyrgyzstan.

LONG JOURNEY

"Go therefore and make disciples of all nations, baptizing them in the name of the Father and of the Son and of the Holy Spirit, teaching them to observe all that I have commanded you. And behold, I am with you always, to the end of the age." (Matthew 28:19–20)

Paul looked over at his wife. Her face looked unnaturally pale.

"How are you doing?" he asked sympathetically.

Melanie looked up at him as her head weakly waved from side-to-side. She vomited into the paper bag she held in her hands. At three months pregnant, this crazy journey across Eastern Europe and Asia was taking a toll on her. Her hands trembled in weakness, and she leaned her head against the train window.

Slowly the days and nights aboard the train passed. The further east the train traveled the more chaotic the stops became. People poured into the train cars selling every kind of local food or product imaginable. And then as the train neared a major border crossing, unsavory characters flooded into the cabins and began pulling panels off the walls. They would fill every nook and cranny with contraband items and products they hoped to sell in order to avoid paying taxes at the border. Then they would replace the panels and disappear.

Paul and Melanie hunkered down in their compartment and tried to stay out of the fray. They wondered what would happen when they reached the border at the next stop.

When the train pulled in to the next town, Paul watched out the window for customs officers, but the uniformed men never bothered to climb aboard the train. They sat down and had tea with the conductor and negotiated a price to let the train through. Paul had heard how things work in this part of the world, but it was hard to be really ready for it.

"Passports!" the border control officers stepped into their compartment.

Paul took out their documents and handed them to the man. He eyed them skeptically.

"What is this?" he asked in coarse Russian.

"These are our visas. We are going to Kyrgyzstan." Paul explained, confused as to what the problem could actually be.

"These are flight visas," the officer stated abruptly. "No good on train."

Melanie looked up at Paul. He knew she was praying. Paul shrugged his shoulders, understanding he would have to play their game to get through this. "Look, all I have is $20."

"That will do," the man snatched the money and left.

Paul released a deep sigh of relief. *They never taught us how to handle this kind of situation in Bible college,* he thought as he chuckled at the memory of his days at the Bible college in Hungary three years earlier. He thought of the stories Paul Lange and Rod Thompson shared during their classes. Now he had plenty of stories of his own—and many more soon to be written—including what life is like when you arrive in Kyrgyzstan penniless.

FINDING A HOME

After a long, five-day journey, the train pulled in to Bishkek, the capital of Kyrgyzstan. The couple had written to several contacts in hopes of finding someone to meet them at the train and help them get acclimated. But they had not received a single reply, so they had no idea what would happen next. As the train neared the station, Paul and Melanie peered out the window at the burnt-out buildings, evidence of the nation's recent political revolution. The heavily Muslim nation was ready for change. Would it be ready for Christ?

Paul and Melanie managed to get all their stuff off the train, wondering what God would do.

"Are you the Billings family?" someone asked through a thick Ukrainian accent.

The couple turned to find Natasha, a Ukrainian missionary with Youth For Christ. She was one person they had written to. Natasha managed to find them a room where they could stay for a few days until they found something more permanent.

Paul walked the streets of the city in awe and expectation of what the Lord might do in such a place. He loved it. Melanie, still struggling with pregnancy fatigue and nausea, did not have the strength or energy to be enthralled just yet. She needed to get through one day at a time.

CHURCH PLANTING

In time, Paul and Melanie settled in their own apartment, and Paul began trying to figure out how to plant a church in a place like this. Kyrgyzstan is known as a closed country when it comes to the gospel, and it appears on lists of nations that persecute believers. Paul knew he would have to approach this wisely. He sought God earnestly about what steps to take. How could he honor the authorities of the land and still fulfill the call of God? Both Paul and Melanie spoke Russian, which helped them communicate with the locals. But everybody gave them a different answer about what was lawful. Finally, Paul decided to go to the source. He set up a meeting with the Minister of Religion and told the man he wanted to start a church.

Although the official did not welcome the idea with open arms, he also did not stop it. He gave Paul a list of things they were forbidden to do and told him how to register the church. Paul immediately began the process of registering a church that ironically, did not yet exist.

Meanwhile, the couple used English classes as a vehicle to get to know people and make friends. In time, a small Bible study formed out of that class, meeting at their apartment.

By the time their baby was born, the couple had settled into a regular routine where they were beginning to see glimpses of God's grace for the Kyrgyz people.

Melanie's parents visited for Titus' birth, giving Paul an opportunity to consult with his father-in-law, a man he greatly admired.

"I think what the Lord is doing with you here is great," George said with confident assurance. Paul appreciated his words of encouragement.

"But I wonder if you're thinking too small," George continued. "I mean, you guys have a little group meeting in your apartment, but why not go rent a room downtown somewhere?"

Paul almost laughed. "We can barely pay the rent on our apartment!" he explained. "I'm not so sure we're ready for something like that."

"Don't limit God, son," the experienced missionary responded.

NO LIMITS

The conversation haunted Paul. *What if George was right?* Paul began looking at places in the city. He stumbled upon an old theater behind a bar and asked about it. The proprietor said he would let them use it for free.

And so the little congregation began to grow. There was no grand explosion of faith, but rather a slow and steady work where God proved faithful, building the church one precious soul at a time.

In the meantime, Paul and Melanie continued the process of trying to register the church as a legal entity.

The process moved at a snail's pace. And until it gained legal recognition, it remained easy prey for the secret police.

The church moved its location around the city as the Lord opened doors. Each time God brought about a move, He timed it to perfection. Within a week's time the owners of the previous location would get a visit from the secret police, questioning the group's activities.

Finally, after nearly four years, Paul managed to complete the process and, miraculously, the church had legal status in Kyrgyzstan.

Other seasoned missionaries joined Paul and Melanie as the church became a pillar in the community. Among them were Melanie's parents, Pam and George Markey, who brought experience and perspective to the young couple and the young church.

The church continued to grow and God raised up leadership within it. Paul found himself continually handing off more and more of the church's responsibilities as the Kyrgyz people grew in faith and service.

JEREMY CAMP AND THE BIG OUTREACH

"Jeremy Camp wants to come here," Paul told his wife after reading the email. "He wants to do a concert here in Bishkek!"

Melanie laughed at the crazy idea of a famous Christian singer from America visiting Kyrgyzstan. "Jeremy Camp, here?"

As far as anyone could recall, there had never been any major evangelistic outreach in Kyrgyzstan... ever!

Paul, Melanie, and their children

Impossible as it seemed, they committed to doing it. They would rent a stadium and fill it with Jeremy's songs of faith and praise. Then Jeremy would openly share the gospel, no holds barred. *It was truly crazy*, Paul thought. *Crazy awesome!*

Most Christians were excited about the event, but few wanted to be openly affiliated with it. The risks were just too high. Paul, along with the church members, agreed to take an open lead. At the end of the concert, Pavel Bolshakov, one of the church elders, boldly proclaimed the love of the Savior in a country where most Christians are afraid to even admit to following Jesus.

The gospel went forth that day to the 10,000 or more Kyrgyz people who filled the stadium. The message rang clear, resounding in people's souls. They heard that there is a God who loves them enough to give His own Son, that they might know Him. The story of grace continued to unfold in the Central Asian stadium that day. It was a new beginning. But for Paul and Melanie, it would prove to be the beginning of the end of their time in Kyrgyzstan.

KICKED OUT

"Our visa renewals have been denied," Paul told his wife after visiting the government office.

"Denied?" Melanie responded. "How is that possible?"

The first news of the rejection felt like a punch in the stomach. Over the past eight years Kyrgyzstan had become their home. They loved the people. How could they leave the church that had become like their very own family? But as they prayed, they began to realize God was telling them their time there was complete. The church could operate, grow, and perhaps even thrive without them. It was time to move on.

And so in 2013, the couple left Kyrgyzstan with heavy yet happy hearts, hearts that brimmed with a supernatural love for Muslim people everywhere. As they prepared to leave, they reflected on how God had allowed them to establish a legal church in a "closed country." And they could not help but wonder how many of these countries viewed as "closed" really are not. It is true that government laws can be difficult. Issues of corruption can be challenging. But the real question is not one of governments and bureaucracies. The question should focus on the people themselves. How open are they to the gospel?

And so the couple was once again in the process of seeking God as to where He would lead them to begin the next chapter in the great story of grace begun on a cross 2,000 years before.

TO THE ENDS OF THE EARTH

"For the eyes of the LORD run to and fro throughout the whole earth, to show Himself strong on behalf of those whose heart is loyal to Him." (2 Chronicles 16:9a–NKJV)

Argaw, Prince, and Paul represent only a few of the wonderful people God has brought through the Bible college in Hungary and sent out to the "ends of the earth."

Who besides God would have chosen to use a small, seemingly insignificant nation to bring His grace to the world?

"It was not because you were more in number than any other people that the LORD set His love on you and chose you, for you were the fewest of all peoples, but it is because the LORD loves you..." (Deuteronomy 7:7–8a)

God spoke these words to His small nation of Israel, a people group who were otherwise insignificant... except that God chose to do something supernatural through them. It is a little like Hungary. In a land unknown by most of the world, God has chosen to work in a special way.

Whether it is through church planting, establishing a Bible college, or mission trips, God is transforming lives. His grace really does change everything. The light of the gospel is piercing through the darkness, one life at a time. And one life is all it takes to be a catalyst for eternal change.

One refugee from Nigeria or Ethiopia could be the very tool God is looking to use for His purposes. One young person, touched by God, could be the driving force for evangelism and church planting in a "closed country." It just takes one individual who is willing to go see what God might do. One person can be a story of grace.

16

A STORY OF GRACE THAT NEVER ENDS

More than two decades beyond the Iron Curtain, those of us who have served as eyewitnesses to the work of God in this part of the world can truly understand how John must have felt when he penned:

Now there are also many other things that Jesus did. Were every one of them to be written, I suppose that the world itself could not contain the books that would be written.
(John 21:25)

God's story of grace can be read in the lives of so many. People who came to serve for a season, those who came to know Christ in this land against all odds, as well as the children born in this generation of change. It would truly be impossible to mention all the lives that contribute to this story of grace.

Joy and me with our kids, Karina, Judah, Hannah, and Niki

But there is over-whelming joy when we look back and see the threads of grace emerge into a fantastic tapestry, a tapestry that artistically weaves, both the good and the bad, into something incredibly beautiful.

We have seen some churches thrive as countless come to Christ. We have seen lives radically transformed. We have also seen some attempts at church planting fizzle out for any number of reasons. We have seen God intervene miraculously to save a dying child. And we have watched and prayed with our whole hearts as another slipped away and went to be with Him in glory. We have seen the Lord reach in and eradicate cancer from one person's body, and let another waste away with the same debilitating disease. Even now, as we compile this book, lives hang in the balance. We do not know how each story will turn out, but we do know that good or bad, life or death, whatever happens will contribute to God's story of grace.

Tamás, the architect, with his wife, Sára, and their family

Over these decades, we have also watched people grow up in the faith. Remember that little girl, Lilla, in the Esztergom church in Chapter 7? Well, she is an adult now and married to the current pastor of Golgota Esztergom.

Árpi, Andrea, and their children

Tamás, the architect who helped renovate the Bible college, now serves as pastor of Golgota Vác, located just north of Budapest. Árpi, who came to Christ while translating for an outreach, survived cancer and the loss of his first wife. God has used him in church planting, pastoring, and now Árpi serves as rector at the Bible college with his wife and two beautiful children. Szilárd Márkus, who began in the ministry just out of college, now oversees a homeless shelter and is the pastor of Golgota Békásmegyer, located in northern Budapest. And let's not forget Jani Németh, the Esztergom skateboarder who in his childhood had never heard of God. Jani grew to become not only a pastor, but also a leader in church planting across Hungary,

Jani, with his wife, Kata, and their children

raising up the next generation with a vision to share the gospel and reach the nation for Christ.

BUILDING FRIENDSHIP

Calvary Chapel was but one of the many groups that came into Eastern Europe right after the Iron Curtain fell. To most we were just another group of Americans, and only time would tell what our fate would be. We kept our heads down and focused on what God had called us to do, which was to reach the unbelievers.

Over time, things changed. We took on not only a Hungarian name, "Golgota," but also a Hungarian flavor as young Hungarian men and women matured in the faith and took over the leadership. The American fingerprint is slowly beginning to disappear, transforming the church into something more Hungarian. Today more than twenty Golgota churches have been established across the country, and sixteen are led by nationals.

As a result of Golgota's tenacity, growth, and integration into Hungarian society, the animosity of the established church has steadily melted away. A very deep affection has replaced that, and it runs both ways. This affection has unified many of the Christian denominations in Hungary, as we have learned to genuinely appreciate each other and the place that we all have in God's work. Some churches worship with an organ and stained glass. Others do it with a piano and hymnbook. Golgota does it with a guitar, jeans, and flip-flops.

THE NATIONS AROUND US

This book has focused primarily on what God is doing in Hungary, but the story of God's grace is evident in the nations around us too. When the Iron Curtain came down many missionaries went into the surrounding nations to bring His grace to those in need of hope.

Ukraine. In 1992, the Lord moved on the heart of an American pastor and his wife who lived in a small town in Indiana. Within a month, they and their eight children moved 5,000 miles from rural America to the overcrowded city of Kiev, Ukraine. George and Pam Markey packed their lives into suitcases, and they and their children were off to bring the love of Jesus to a country that had recently declared its independence from the Soviet Bloc. Throughout Ukraine, breadlines were customary and hope was in desperate shortage. But at the same time God was working through Greg Opean in Hungary, He was using George Markey and his family in Ukraine. As this unique missions "team" of ten unlikely Americans arrived in Ukraine, not speaking a word of Russian, God began to use them to impact this nation for Christ.

What God has done and is doing in Ukraine is another story of grace. The Calvary Chapel churches in Ukraine are called Golgofa. To date, eighteen churches have been planted, many of them led by nationals today.

Romania. Not long after Mike Harris, Greg Opean, and Rod Thompson went to Yugoslavia and Hungary, God called others like them into Romania. Just a few years after the Christmas Day execution of the brutal dictator

Nicolae Ceaușescu, missionaries headed in to bring a message of hope and grace. Today, nine churches have been established.

Former Yugoslavia. In 1991, Croatia and Slovenia broke away from Yugoslavia to form their own republics, resulting in a bloody war. By January of 1992, Macedonia declared its independence, and in April, Bosnia-Herzegovina did the same. A brutal war raged across Bosnia-Herzegovina and Croatia. In the midst of war, many brave Christians worked to bring the gospel to these nations. Those pioneers laid the groundwork for the churches that have been planted in Slovenia, Croatia, and Serbia.

Without Walls, Without Borders. Of course, regardless of nationality, many in the former Soviet Bloc still hesitate to set foot in anything called a church. With the expectation of reaching these wounded souls, the Internet has become a bedrock tool. In Hungary, Golgota has set up an Internet radio station with Christian music, Bible teachings, and devotionals, and more than 5,000 folks tune in each month. People from all over Hungary and the Hungarian-speaking world watch our services live on the Internet, logging in every week to hear the Word.

NEVER ENDING STORY

This story of grace does not end here. It has only just begun, and its chapters will continue to unfold in the years, decades, and even centuries to come.

Throughout Scripture, we see God using the insignificant for His most significant purposes. We are witnessing how God is using a tiny country, obscure to the rest of the world, as His tool for the nations.

God specializes in making something out of nothing. From the greatest, most talented person to the poor and lowly, every living, breathing human being has the potential to play a part in His great story of grace for this world. All it takes is the simple willingness to "go and see what the Lord will do."

Are you ready to let the Author and Finisher of our faith write your story of grace?

ABOUT TRUDY CHUN

Trudy Chun is a writer, author, and missionary. She began as a political writer in Washington, and later served as editor of Concerned Women for America's *Family Voice* magazine. Her writing has appeared in *Cup of Comfort for Adoptive Families*, *Cup of Comfort for a Better World*, and *Breakpoint Worldview* magazine, as well as other publications. She is the author of *Love&Ashes*, a women's Bible study, and the *BuddhaPest*, a young adult novel, both available on amazon.com.

Trudy and her family live in eastern Hungary where she and her husband minister to orphans and refugees with GoodSports International, as they raise their three third-culture kids.

Visit confessionsofamissionarywife.blogspot.com and learn about GoodSports at goodsportsinternational.org.